SP?T the BULLSH*T
TRIVIA CHALLENGE

FIND THE LIES (and Learn the Truth) from Science, History, Sports, Pop Culture, and More!

NEIL PATRICK STEWART

Adams Media
New York   London   Toronto   Sydney   New Delhi

A adams media

Adams Media
An Imprint of
Simon & Schuster, LLC
100 Technology Center Drive
Stoughton, Massachusetts
02072

First Adams Media hardcover
edition February 2024

ADAMS MEDIA and colophon
are registered trademarks of
Simon & Schuster, LLC.

Simon & Schuster: Celebrating
100 Years of Publishing in 2024

For information about special
discounts for bulk purchases,
please contact Simon &
Schuster Special Sales at
1-866-506-1949 or
business@simonandschuster.com.

The Simon & Schuster Speakers
Bureau can bring authors to your
live event. For more information
or to book an event, contact
the Simon & Schuster Speakers
Bureau at 1-866-248-3049
or visit our website at
www.simonspeakers.com.

Interior design by Julia Jacintho
Interior images © 123RF;
Getty Images
Beatles illustration by
Claudia Wolf

Manufactured in the United
States of America

1 2023

Library of Congress Cataloging-
in-Publication Data
Names: Stewart, Neil Patrick,
author.
Title: Spot the bullsh*t trivia
challenge / Neil Patrick Stewart.
Description: First Adams Media
hardcover edition. | Stoughton,
Massachusetts: Adams Media,
2024. | Includes index.
Identifiers: LCCN 2023037729 |
ISBN 9781507221891 (hc) |
ISBN 9781507221907 (ebook)
Subjects: LCSH: Questions and
answers. | Curiosities and wonders.
Classification: LCC GV1507.Q5
S76 2024 | DDC 001--dc23/
eng/20231019
LC record available at
https://lccn.loc.gov/2023037729

ISBN 978-1-5072-2189-1
ISBN 978-1-5072-2190-7
(ebook)

Contains material adapted from
the following title published
by Adams Media, an Imprint of
Simon & Schuster, LLC: *Fact.
Fact. Bullsh*t!* by Neil Patrick
Stewart, copyright © 2011, ISBN
978-1-4405-2553-7.

contents

CHAPTER FOUR
Weird Science...131

CHAPTER FIVE
Sports and
Other Activities...171

CHAPTER SIX
Florilegium,
Omnium-Gatherum,
and Gallimaufry...213

Introduction

Did you know that…sliced bread loaves became popular in 1937? Manatees used to be mistaken for mermaids? Uranus has only been visited once?

Did you also know that one of these "facts" is total and complete bullsh*t?

*Spot the Bullsh*t Trivia Challenge* puts your knowledge of obscure facts to the test! This fun book has more than two hundred true facts—and more than one hundred lies—about everything from ligers to zombies to high-fructose corn syrup (oh my!). Each challenge includes three statements about the same fun subject, of which *two are true and one is a lie*. It's your job to spot the bullsh*t! Test yourself and your friends, and you're guaranteed to buy some of these complete lies—hook, line, and sinker. Whether you're interested in elephants or Rubik's Cubes or anything in between, there's a trivia challenge for everyone!

Dive into a mountain of data on a plethora of topics, ranging from:

- **Kingdom Animalia:** Where you'll learn facts about some of the most dangerous, common, or elusive species in the world.

- **Pop Culture:** Where you'll puzzle over favorite brands, celebrities, and media.

- **Everything Edible:** Where you'll sink your teeth into facts and fictions about the food around you.

- **Weird Science:** Where you'll follow your scientific method to discover the truths of daily life and the universe.

- **Sports and Other Activities:** Where you'll cheer over the facts in your athletic fandom.

- **Florilegium, Omnium-Gatherum, and Gallimaufry:** Where you'll learn miscellaneous facts that had no other home in this book.

Each of these topics has pages of fun bullsh*t to explore, and how you go through these challenges is up to you: Do one subject at a time or have an afternoon trivia marathon! With each challenge, lock in your final answer, then turn the page to find out if your educated guess was backed up by fact. The back of each page includes descriptions about why each choice is fact or bullsh*t.

What are you waiting for? Flip the page and start your fun-fueled challenge now. More often than not, you'll be surprised at the bullsh*t you find.

CHAPTER ONE

**Kingdom
Animalia**

"FACTS":
The Giraffe!

1 Lugging around that long neck is tiring! Giraffes are one of the sleepiest mammals around; they average a whopping fifteen hours of sleep per twenty-four-hour period. They're great at hiding it, however: They only sleep standing up.

2 It was originally called a "cameleopard." Fourteenth-century Romans came up with the name because they thought the beast looked like a cross between a camel and a leopard. The Afrikaans language still takes its cues from the Romans, calling the giraffe the *kameelperd*.

3 Giraffes need a serious ticker to get blood up those long necks to their brains: A giraffe's heart weighs up to 25 pounds—and can be more than 2 feet long.

1 Bullsh*t!

In fact, the opposite is true. Giraffes need less sleep than most other mammals, and sometimes they sleep as little as ten minutes in a given day. On average, they sleep between thirty and 120 minutes daily. While they can sleep standing up, they also curl up on the ground and sleep with their head resting on their own rump. Giraffes often doze in very short bursts, keeping their ears perked to listen for predators.

2 **Fact.** Those silly Romans! Have you ever seen a camel or a leopard with a 6-foot neck?

3 **Fact.** A giraffe's heart has special valves to regulate blood pressure, which changes each time its head is raised or lowered (like when eating from a tree or drinking from a spring). Without its specialized heart, raising its head would lead to such a drastic change in blood pressure that the giraffe would faint.

"FACTS":
The Dog!

1 The dog is the most widely kept companion animal in human history. There is approximately one dog for every seventeen people on Earth. In the United States, we have dog fever: There is one dog for every four people.

2 The fox is actually a kind of dog. Domesticated silver foxes that behave just like normal dogs were bred in painstaking selective-breeding experiments that were started sixty years ago by Soviet scientists.

3 A dog's sense of smell is so well developed that it can perceive odors at concentrations sixty times lower than a human can.

1 **Fact.** It is estimated that there are 471 million pet dogs on the planet, and 8 billion people. That's one dog for every 16.9851 people. We'll call that seventeen. Roughly 335 million people live in the US, and approximately 89.7 million pet dogs. That's one dog for every 3.7346 people. We'll call that four. Cats are less popular than dogs in the US (one pet cat for every 5.75 people), and dogs have been domesticated by humans for more than 12,000 years (some experts put it closer to 100,000), whereas cats became domesticated roughly 5,000 years ago.

2 **Fact.** The project was set up in 1959 by Soviet scientist Dmitri Belyaev. The foxes were selected based on tame behavior for over forty generations, and the project produced foxes that were extremely friendly toward humans, wagged their tails, and liked to lick faces. The term "dog" can be used to refer to any member of the family Canidae. Under this definition, foxes, wolves, jackals, and dingoes are all dogs. The prairie dog is not, in fact, a dog. (Neither is the dogfish.)

3 # Bullsh*t!

The dog's ability to smell should be considered a superpower. Dogs can perceive odors at concentrations nearly 100 million times lower than a human. Your dog's cold, wet nose also aids its sense of smell: The wetness helps it determine the direction of the air current, which in turn helps it determine the direction a smell is coming from.

"FACTS":
The Falcon!

1 Peregrine falcons are exceedingly rare and critically endangered, with numerous conservation efforts in full swing to keep them around. Unfortunately, peregrines are among the slowest-moving birds of prey and are consistently outperformed in their habitat.

2 All kestrels (such as the Madagascar kestrel and the gray kestrel), hobbies (such as the African hobby and the Oriental hobby), and merlins (such as the black merlin and the prairie merlin) are falcons. All falcons (such as the red-necked falcon and the bat falcon) are raptors. Eagles, hawks, and vultures are also raptors.

3 A groundbreaking gene study published in 2008 suggests that falcons are actually more closely related to parrots and songbirds than to hawks or eagles.

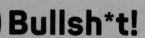

1 Bullsh*t!

Peregrine falcons are neither rare nor endangered. On the contrary, they can be found nearly everywhere on the planet, from the highest mountains to the densest tropics. They are the most widespread bird of prey. They are also hands-down the fastest animal in the world, having been clocked at 240 miles per hour during a dive.

2 **Fact.** The term "raptor" loosely refers to birds of prey that hunt during the day, whereas birds of prey that hunt at night are called owls. Kestrels, hobbies, and merlins are all members of the genus *Falco* and the order Falconiformes, making them falcons.

3 **Fact.** The finding, sponsored by the National Science Foundation's Assembling the Tree of Life initiative, is counter to the assumptions made by ornithologists for decades. Falcons have the same curved beak as their parrot and songbird counterparts, but they have evolved to be strong predators (just like hawks and eagles).

"FACTS":
The Duck-Billed Platypus!

1 The platypus was first discovered by European explorers in 1849, and early British settlers in Australia (its native environment) called it a beaverduck. The plural of platypus is "platypi."

2 Besides being one of just a few species of mammals that lay eggs, the platypus is also one of a very few species of mammals that are actually venomous! A male platypus has a spur above the foot in each hind leg that can inject venom produced by a gland in its thigh.

3 A mother platypus will nurse her young, but not with help from her nipples: She doesn't have any. Instead, milk is secreted through pores in her abdomen, which the babies scrape up with their bills.

Bullsh*t!

European explorers discovered the animal in 1798, and British settlers commonly referred to the platypus by many names, including the watermole, duckbill, and duckmole, but not beaverduck. While colloquially used, "platypi" is not a correct pluralized form of platypus. There is no universally agreed-upon plural form because both "platypus" and "platypuses" are thought to be correct in different circles.

Fact. The spur is about 15 millimeters long, and a platypus will use it to defend itself. The gland in the thigh is called the crural gland. While not deadly to humans, the venom can cause quite a bit of discomfort. The best way to pick up a platypus and not get poisoned is by the tip of the tail. Other venomous mammals are the Eurasian water shrew and the European mole.

Fact. While she does have mammary glands, a female platypus has no teats. It's a good thing too—a baby platypus is born with a full set of teeth. The teeth fall out after a couple of weeks.

"FACTS":
The Frog!

1 Many people get frogs and toads confused, but they are, in fact, two completely separate taxonomic groups from different orders and families. The resemblance between the two is a biological marvel since you'd have to go way back on the evolutionary timeline to find a common ancestor.

2 Frogs of the genus *Ceratophrys* are known as "Pacman frogs" because of their huge mouths and round shape, as well as their tendency to try to swallow anything that they can fit their prodigious mouths around, including fish, mice, lizards, and even birds.

3 Frogs are biological wonders: They have no external ears, a great many can breathe and drink through their skin, and most frogs actually have teeth.

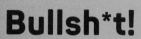

1 Bullsh*t!

Taxonomy makes no distinction between frogs and toads. In fact, contrary to widely held belief, all toads are frogs. This explains why they resemble one another so closely! All frogs and toads are amphibians of the order Anura, and many species of frog and toad come from the same family.

2 **Fact.** A Pacman frog will sometimes even try to swallow things it *can't* get its mouth around, such as rodents twice its size. Unfortunately, this practice typically causes the frog to suffocate and die. Such frogs are fearless, and some will actually leap at and attack anything that threatens them, even if vastly overmatched, such as a human. Pacman frogs will even try to swallow other Pacman frogs, including their mates. For this reason, pet stores helpfully suggest you keep them in separate tanks.

3 **Fact.** Rather than ears, frogs have tympanums, a structure similar to a drumhead; however, frogs do have inner ears. A frog's skin is water permeable, which means water can be absorbed through the skin. Many frogs absorb oxygen in the same way. The permeable skin does leave frogs vulnerable to drying out, which is why we often observe frogs crouching in water. Most frogs actually do have teeth, generally in the form of one row of upper teeth, or maxillary teeth. They often have teeth further back on the roof of their mouths as well, or vomerine teeth. Frogs never have lower teeth. The teeth aren't used to chew—frogs generally swallow their food whole.

"FACTS":
The
Cockroach!

1 The cockroach is so hardy that some species can survive without food for a month, can be submerged for forty-five minutes or more without drowning, can regenerate lost limbs, and can even walk away after being nuked in a microwave.

2 The green banana cockroach is a popular pet because of its bright green color and ability to fly, while the Florida woods cockroach is not because of its ability to emit a very persistent, very foul odor.

3 The Central American giant cave cockroach is the heaviest insect in the world: It routinely grows to lengths of 5 inches or more and can weigh in at nearly 60 grams, or about as much as eleven US quarters.

1 **Fact.** Cockroaches truly are incredible little creatures. Perhaps most shocking is their ability to sometimes survive a microwave oven at full blast. There
are two main explanations for this phenomenon:
First, roaches have very little water in their physical
makeup. Microwave radiation causes water molecules
in our TV dinners to vibrate, which causes friction
and, consequently, heat. Second, microwave ovens
do not spread their heating power uniformly throughout the chamber. Many have carousels to keep the
food moving through the most intense focus points
of the heat. A savvy cockroach can actually flee to
the coolest parts of the microwave.

2 **Fact.** The green banana cockroach is lime green and
generally not regarded as a pest since they prefer
to remain outdoors. They are very strong flyers. The
Florida woods cockroach is often called a palmetto
bug or a skunk roach.

3 # Bullsh*t!

The heaviest insect in the world is the goliath beetle, native to Africa, which can grow to more than
4 inches long and weigh in at 100 grams or more
(about the weight of a newborn kitten). The heaviest
cockroach is the giant burrowing cockroach, which
can reach 3.5 inches in length, and weigh in at 30
grams. The Central American giant cave cockroach
routinely grows to the same length but is nowhere
near as heavy.

"FACTS":
The
Hummingbird!

1 The world's smallest bird is the bee hummingbird, native to Cuba. The bee hummingbird is the same length as the short side of a standard business card and weighs less than one.

2 Hummingbirds have the highest metabolism of any living animal. The fastest heart rate ever measured in a hummingbird is 450 beats per minute. Fast living means fast dying: Hummingbirds have a lifespan of about a year.

3 Hummingbirds hover by beating their wings at an extremely high velocity—often as fast as 100 beats per second. Hummingbirds routinely fly at 30 miles per hour and can dive at 60 miles per hour. They are the only species of bird that can fly backward.

1 **Fact.** The bee hummingbird is less than 2 inches long and weighs less than 2 grams. That's less than the weight of a dime, or the combined weight of two $1 bills! A bee hummingbird's nest is about 1 inch wide.

2 # Bullsh*t!

You could only claim that hummingbirds have the highest metabolism of any animal if you exclude insects. A blue-throated hummingbird was once measured to have a heart rate of 1,260 beats per minute. Such a high metabolism means humming-birds have to consume several times their weight in nectar per day and are constantly hours away from death by starvation. Still, they soldier on and are longevity wonders when you consider their incredible metabolic rate. Average American hum-mingbirds live for three to five years, and several species routinely live for longer than a decade. One hummingbird in captivity lived for seventeen years.

3 **Fact.** There is actually quite a range in wing beats per second—the wings of the giant hummingbird beat about nine times per second; medium-sized species beat around twenty times per second; while the small-est species can get up to one hundred. Hummingbirds can rotate their wings and actually get power from both the upstroke and the downstroke. As a consequence, they can hover and fly side to side, as well as forward and backward. No other birds can do this; physicists are actively studying hummingbirds in hopes of improving our own understanding of aerodynamics.

"FACTS":
The Panda!

1 Pandas are the most expensive animals to keep in American zoos. They are five times more costly than the elephant, which is the second most expensive.

2 Pandas, like all bears, are members of the scientific family Muridae. Their closest evolutionary relatives are dogs, of the family Canidae. The panda's closest living relative is *Ailurus fulgens*, or the red panda, which is extremely dog-like.

3 Pandas are notoriously reluctant to mate in captivity. Many outside-the-box methods to encourage reproduction have been attempted, including showing the lazy bears "panda porn" and even dosing them with Viagra.

1 **Fact.** The Chinese government regularly charges foreign zoos $1 million per year per panda on loan. If cubs are born, then China increases the price by another $500,000 or so. Pandas require upwards of 80 pounds of bamboo per day for their diet, which only adds to the price tag.

2 # Bullsh*t!

Pandas, like all bears, are members of the scientific family Ursidae. (Muridae are mice.) Ursidae's closest relatives are the superfamily Pinnipedia, which, believe it or not, are comprised of seals, walruses, and sea lions. The panda's closest living relative is the South American spectacled bear. Dogs, walruses, bears, and skunks are all members of the suborder Caniformia, which means that bears and dogs are more closely related to each other than they are to other mammals, such as rodents, cats, kangaroos, and humans. Red pandas are not bears at all.

3 **Fact.** Panda breeders in China have all but torn their hair out in search of ways to encourage copulation. Among the many things they have tried are artificial insemination, special herbs, Viagra, and showing videos of pandas mating, popularly referred to as "panda porn."

"FACTS":
The Cow!

1 The sport of cow tipping has been debunked as being largely myth. It would be impossible for one or two people to tip over a full-sized, healthy cow. Five people could conceivably do it, but only if the cow were rigid and completely unresponsive, which is unlikely, as cows do not sleep standing up.

2 Cows have four stomachs, each of which perform a unique digestive function. They are called the triclinium, the caldarium, the apodyterium, and the puteus. The triclinium is the largest.

3 Cattle use more than 35 percent of the world's habitable land and are one of the biggest contributors to harmful greenhouse gases in our atmosphere, even ahead of cars! The majority of the gas released comes from cow burps, flatulence, and poop.

1 **Fact.** Cows do not sleep standing up, but they can doze off while chewing their cud. Still, cows are wary and easily disturbed, so sneaking up on one would be particularly difficult. According to a 2005 study by zoologists, tipping over a cow would require 2,910 newtons of force, or the equivalent of 4.43 people. This would require the cow to be as still as a statue. Cows, like most animals on legs, would brace themselves against the force, which would make them even more difficult to tip.

2 # Bullsh*t!

Technically, cows have one stomach with four compartments. They are called the rumen, the reticulum, the omasum, and the abomasum. The rumen is the largest. Triclinium, caldarium, apodyterium, and puteus are all architectural features of ancient Roman bathhouses.

3 **Fact.** There are an estimated 1.5 billion cattle in the world and roughly 8 billion people. The automotive industry produces rawer CO_2 than livestock, but if you measure CO_2-equivalent gases, cattle production as a whole produces 14.5 percent of human-related greenhouse gases released into our atmosphere, which is more than cars. The cow-produced methane comes from "enteric fermentation," which is science speak for burps and gas, and the nitrous oxide comes from manure.

"FACTS":
The
Earthworm!

1 Earthworms are hermaphrodites and have both testes
and ovaries. However, an earthworm cannot fertilize itself.

2 A study by Rothamsted Research suggests that rich
farmland can have as many as 1,750,000 earthworms
per acre, which means, on a dairy farm, the worms
below can easily outweigh the livestock above.

3 The giant Palouse earthworm from Washington state
is the world's longest species of earthworm, regularly
growing to lengths of up to 7 feet.

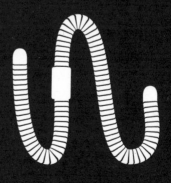

1 **Fact.** Earthworms do copulate with each other to reproduce. When they do, both individuals release sperm to fertilize the other's eggs. Earthworms have a thick band, called a clitellum, which oozes a thick fluid after copulation to make a cocoon. The earthworm deposits its own eggs and the other worm's sperm into the cocoon. Some types of earthworms can reproduce by themselves via parthenogenesis, but this process is asexual and produces a clone.

2 **Fact.** Darwin, in his time, was a great student of the earthworm. He suggested that each acre of garden land contained 53,000 worms, a figure that Rothamsted Research has significantly increased with their recent findings. According to Rothamsted, even poor soil can have as many as 250,000 worms per acre.

3 # Bullsh*t!

The world's longest earthworms are African giant earthworms, which have been recorded to grow as long as 22 feet and can weigh in at more than 3 pounds. The giant Palouse earthworm is still a shocking specimen—they are albino, sometimes more than an inch thick, and can grow up to 3½ feet long.

"FACTS":
The Elephant!

1 Elephants are the only surviving members of the scientific order Proboscidea, which once included the 26-foot-long *Stegodon*, the *Platybelodon* with its huge shovel-shaped tusks, the *Cuvieronius* with its long spiral-shaped tusks, the *Anancus* with tusks as long as its body, the huge and shaggy woolly mammoth, and the similarly hairy American mastodon.

2 We often see elephants as gentle giants, but in truth, they are often very aggressive, violent, and dangerous. Recently, in India, elephants have mounted raids against human villages, killing hundreds of people.

3 While the human body contains approximately 2,000 major muscles, there are nearly 10,000 muscles in an elephant's trunk alone!

1 **Fact.** Asian and African elephants are the only members left of what was a big, diverse family of enormous mammals. In English, we often facetiously use the term "proboscis" to mean nose, but it actually means "an elongated appendage on the head of an animal." A butterfly has a proboscis, as does an elephant.

2 **Fact.** Elephants have been killing people and destroying villages in India, and, scarily, the incidents appear to be increasing in frequency. Many experts believe that the attacks are actually vindictive—a response to poaching and destruction of their habitat. Elephant violence and aggression aren't new though. Trained war elephants were used in battle by the Greek general Pyrrhus of Epirus and the Carthaginian military commander Hannibal.

3 # Bullsh*t!

In terms of major muscles, an elephant's trunk has 40,000, and broken up into the individual muscle units, it has more than 100,000! The human body only has between 600 and 900 major muscles, depending on your criteria. A full-sized elephant, with its trunk alone, can lift objects in the neighborhood of 500 pounds. The trunk is also dexterous and sensitive enough to pick a single blade of grass or retrieve a coin from the ground.

"FACTS":
The Manatee!

1 Manatees belong to the order Sirenia, which comes from the Latin *syreni*, meaning "mermaid." The name "manatee" is believed to be derived from the Carib word *manati*, which means "breast."

2 A manatee can grow as long as 12 feet and can weigh nearly 4,000 pounds! It makes sense that they can be so large—their closest living relative is the elephant.

3 While Florida manatees typically swim too deep to be threatened by recreational boat traffic, there have been a handful of cases where manatees have been injured by collisions with hulls and propellers. Recently, an individual manatee was discovered with scar patterns from three separate boat collisions (a record!).

1 **Fact.** It's a common theory that the mermaid sightings of Christopher Columbus's day were, in fact, sea cow sightings. Manatees do have mammary glands near their armpits.

2 **Fact.** Manatees are mammals and are believed to have evolved from four-legged land creatures some 60 million years ago. They are closely related to the order Proboscidea (the elephants) as well as the order Hyracoidea (the hyraxes). Manatees have a prehensile upper lip that shows similar properties to an elephant trunk, though it's not nearly as long! Though manatees can grow to be 12 feet long and weigh nearly 4,000 pounds, an average one would be a little over 9 feet long and weigh around 1,000 pounds.

3 # Bullsh*t!

Manatees typically graze at a depth of 3 to 6 feet, and are frequently mutilated, maimed, and occasionally killed by collisions with boats and boat propellers. It is common to discover manatees bearing the scar patterns of more than ten separate boat or propeller collisions, and one was discovered with evidence of more than fifty separate collisions. Many of these creatures have been observed with gruesome disfigurements due to the slicing and dicing of motorboat propellers, including gaping wounds, severed tails, and exposed lungs. The manatees are tough, however, and amazingly, often survive.

"FACTS": The Tyrannosaurus!

1 *Tyrannosaurus rex* was a coelurosaur of the Saurischia order and of the suborder Theropoda, from which all modern birds evolved. Cousins to the *Tyrannosaurus*, all modern birds are dinosaurs.

2 The *Tyrannosaurus* was one of the largest land carnivores ever and could grow to over 40 feet long and 13 feet tall at the hip. There were larger bipedal carnivores, however, including the *Spinosaurus* and the *Giganotosaurus*, both of which looked very similar to *T. rex*.

3 *T. rex* was dominant during the Jurassic period, which lasted from about 250 million to 200 million years ago and saw the dawn of dinosaurs.

1 **Fact.** Although there is still some token scientific dissent to the idea, most paleontologists now agree that birds are avian dinosaurs. The evidence is strong enough now that we feel confident calling it truth. *T. rex* was a member of Coelurosauria, which is a group ("clade") of theropod dinosaurs closely related to birds. *T. rex* was a saurischian, which means "lizard-hipped." All carnivorous dinosaurs were saurischians. Finally, *Tyrannosaurus* was a theropod, which describes both a suborder of carnivorous saurischian dinosaurs and the clade of those dinosaurs and their descendants, including birds.

2 **Fact.** The *Giganotosaurus* was slightly larger than *Tyrannosaurus*, but its brain was half as big. *Spinosaurus* was bigger than both *Tyrannosaurus* and *Giganotosaurus* and had a big, scary "sail" of elongated spinal bones.

3 # Bullsh*t!

Although the movie *Jurassic Park* implies otherwise, *Tyrannosaurus* did not live during the Jurassic period. It lived during the Cretaceous period. The Triassic period, not the Jurassic, was 250 to 200 million years ago, and the first dinosaurs appeared then. The Jurassic was about 200 to 145 million years ago, and the Cretaceous was about 145 to 65 million years ago. All three periods make up the Mesozoic era (or the Age of Reptiles). *T. rex* existed during the tail end of the Cretaceous, about 67 million years ago, and was one of the last non-avian dinosaurs on earth before the major extinction event.

"FACTS":
The Swan!

1 The largest native North American bird (by weight and length) is the trumpeter swan, which can tip the scales at 38 pounds, can grow to be 6 feet long, and have a nearly 10-foot wingspan. It is the largest waterfowl on Earth.

2 Swans may look pure, but they are actually quite promiscuous, mating often and with many partners. Most species of swan are polygamous: During a breeding season, a female will mate with several males, with the result that a single clutch of eggs could have several fathers.

3 In England, all unmarked mute swans are technically property of the Crown. There is an annual ceremonial swan census on the River Thames called "Swan Upping." A crew of Royal Swan Uppers in scarlet uniforms row for five days while counting swans and are led by a man with the prestigious title of "the King's Swan Marker."

1 **Fact.** Turkeys can be heavier, and the California condor can have a wider wingspan, but the trumpeter swan is larger than both when you count all factors. The largest bird in the world is the ostrich, which can grow to 9 feet tall and weigh 400 pounds. The largest bird ever was the elephant bird of Madagascar, now extinct, which could have weighed up to 900 pounds and was regularly more than 10 feet tall.

2 Bullsh*t!

Swans have long been one of the shining examples of monogamy in the animal kingdom. A swan will form a bond with one partner that can last for many years and sometimes for life. This is one of the main reasons why swans are a symbol of love. Our cherished view of the sanctity of swan "marriage" is under attack, however, as studies have shown swan "divorce" to be more common than previously thought. An added fun fact: Mute swans have been documented to form same-sex partnerships.

3 **Fact.** The tradition began in the twelfth century, when swans were a rare and royal delicacy for the dinner table. Today, the tradition is upheld for the sake of conservation. When the Royal Swan Uppers pass Windsor Castle, the rowers stand at attention in the boat and salute "His Majesty the King, Seigneur of the Swans."

"FACTS":
The Otter!

1 Otters are in the same biological family as badgers, polecats, weasels, stoats, minks, and wolverines.

2 Giant otters, also known as "river dogs," are native to the San Jorge Gulf, off the coast of Argentina. A fully grown male giant otter is typically between 7 and 8 feet long and will weigh upwards of 300 pounds!

3 Sea otters have the thickest fur of any animal in the world, boasting between 600,000 and 1 million hairs per square inch. Altogether, each sea otter has around 800 million hairs on its body.

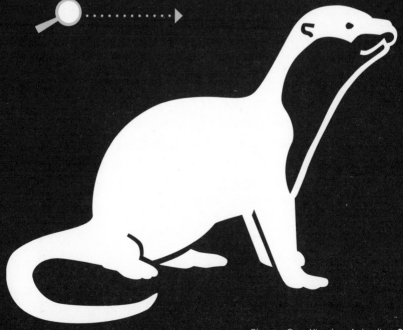

1 **Fact.** Otters and the others are members of the family Mustelidae, from the Latin *mustela*, for "weasel." Although they all share the same family, biologists believe otters are most closely related to minks and weasels.

2 # Bullsh*t!

Don't be ridiculous. Giant otters, also known as "water dogs"—or "river wolves" in South America—aren't that giant. They're native to the Amazon River in the northern half of South America. Males are about 5 feet long and weigh about 80 pounds. There are reports of giant otter skins measuring over 7 feet, but this size is not typical and has not been seen in quite some time, likely a result of the big guys being poached. Sea otters often weigh more than giant otters, tipping the scales at up to 100 pounds.

3 **Fact.** If you're wondering just how hairy that really is, humans typically have about 100,000 to 150,000 hairs on their whole head. Sea otters' fur is so thick that their skin doesn't get wet when they swim. This makes up for the fact that they have no blubber to keep them warm like seals do. Sea otters are one of the only non-primate species of mammal in the world that uses tools. They use rocks to break open the shells of clams, mussels, snails, and crabs to get to the tasty morsels inside.

"FACTS":
The Shark!

1 The smallest species of shark is the dwarf lanternshark, which is typically between 6 and 7 inches long. The largest is the whale shark, which can grow longer than 60 feet and is also the largest existing species of fish.

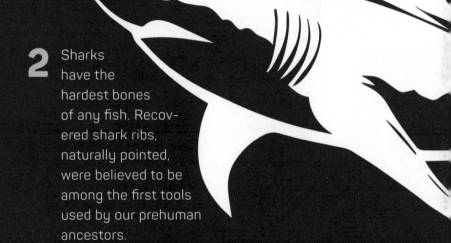

2 Sharks have the hardest bones of any fish. Recovered shark ribs, naturally pointed, were believed to be among the first tools used by our prehuman ancestors.

3 One of the rarest species of fish in the sea is the megamouth shark, which was only discovered in 1976. In the decades since then, there have been fewer than 300 sightings or specimens reported. Scientists still know very little about the big, flabby bottom-feeder.

1 **Fact.** The longest-known dwarf lanternshark was 8.3 inches. These little guys have only been spotted in a relatively small area of the Caribbean, off the coasts of Colombia and Venezuela. The longest-known whale shark was measured at 61.7 feet. The heaviest recorded weighed in at 47,000 pounds!

2 # Bullsh*t!

Sharks, like rays and skates, are cartilaginous fish—a shark skeleton has no bone and is made up of cartilage and connective tissue, roughly half the density of bone. Sharks are very unique in this way: The vast majority of fish are Osteichthyes, which do have bony skeletons. On top of that, sharks have no rib cage at all. Because of this, a shark on land would be in great danger of being crushed by its own body weight.

3 **Fact.** The megamouth is aptly named, since it is characterized by its large head and big, rubbery lips. By 2022, only 273 confirmed sightings had been reported of the megamouth, making it a rare fish indeed. In 2022, a video of two of these sharks socializing near the surface of the water gained a lot of attention. These two fish were seemingly found spending some "quality time" together.

"FACTS":
The Koala!

1 Koalas are herbaceous omnivores, native to Western Australia and Tasmania. Dependent on the rainforest for survival, they are a critically endangered species.

2 The male koala has a bifurcated penis (two for the price of one!), and female koalas have two lateral vaginas and two uteri.

3 Koalas sleep between sixteen and twenty-two hours per day because of their incredibly slow metabolism and their poor diet. They spend between two and five hours a day eating.

1 Bullsh*t!

Koalas live in woodlands, not rainforests. They are native to eastern and southern Australia and are not found in Western Australia or Tasmania. Koalas are not herbaceous (this word describes plants), and they are not omnivores but herbivores. They are also not critically endangered, but due to wildfires, they are endangered and have fewer than 58,000 individuals in the wild.

2 **Fact.** Strange but true. Most male marsupials have some version of this "double" penis. Female koalas have a "vaginal apparatus" that consists of two lateral vaginas, each connected to a separate uterus.

3 **Fact.** Koalas subsist entirely on leaves, their favorite being eucalyptus leaves. It is an odd choice, since eucalyptus leaves are low in protein and high in toxins and indigestible fibrous matter. Having a low metabolism and sleeping quite a bit help koalas conserve the massive amount of energy they need to digest and process such difficult food.

"FACTS":
The Liger!

1 Hybrid cats such as the liger (a cross between a male tiger and a lioness) are completely infertile. In the wild, a liger could never happen: It takes human intervention, veterinary attention, and careful planning in captivity to create the delicate conditions appropriate for a lion and tiger to successfully mate.

2 Ligers are the largest cats in the world. Hercules, a 900-plus pound, 12-foot-long liger from South Carolina, holds the Guinness World Record for biggest living cat and is larger than both his parents *combined*.

3 Ligers are far from alone in the hybrid big-cat animal kingdom. There have been confirmed cases of jaglions, liguars, leoliguars, jagupards, leguars, lijaguleps, leopons, lipards, leoligulors, and tigards.

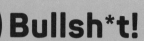

Bullsh*t!

Ligers and their counterparts, tiglons, were long thought to be infertile, but this turns out to be incorrect. Male ligers and tiglons are sterile, but females are often fertile. In one example, a 1975 pairing between a lion and a female liger resulted in a cub (referred to as a liliger) that was successfully raised to adulthood. The liger is a hybrid cross between a male lion and a tigress. A male tiger and a lioness's offspring is a tiglon. Ligers are much more common in zoos and parks today than tiglons. It does not take human intervention or careful planning for ligers to be produced. In fact, most of the ligers in captivity were produced by accident. In the wild, lion and tiger mating is extremely unlikely, mainly because lion and tiger habitats, in general, don't overlap. But it *could* happen, and many biologists think it has.

2 **Fact.** Ligers' huge size is a result of hybrid vigor, which means Hercules inherited the best traits from both species. Hercules is said to be able to run at 50 miles per hour and to eat more than 25 pounds of meat a day.

3 **Fact.** All are very real. The lijagulep is the result of a male lion mating with a female jagupard or leguar, and the leoligulor is the result of a fertile male leopon mating with a liguar. Zebroids (zebra and horse), pizzly bears (polar bear and grizzly bear), and wholpins (dolphin and false killer whale) are all real too.

"FACTS":
The Unicorn!

1 While the mythical unicorn never existed, the single-horned monoceros did. Last observed by Dutch biologist Petrus Plancius in 1613, sightings of the monoceros, a nomadic antilocaprid most closely related to the giraffe, were extremely rare and usually occurred at night.

2 In 1663, in Germany's Harz Mountains, a fossilized skeleton was constructed that appeared to be a unicorn. It was assembled by scientist and inventor Otto von Guericke and later examined by philosopher and mathematician Gottfried Leibniz, both of whom concluded that it was, in fact, a unicorn.

3 A "unicorn bull," with a large, single horn growing out of the middle of its head, was the wonder of a 1933 cow herd. The "unicorn" was the undisputed leader of all the other bulls, and it had the same gentle, docile temperament that is often attributed to the mythical unicorn.

1 Bullsh*t!

Monoceros, first observed by Dutch cartographer Petrus Plancius in 1612 or 1613, is a constellation on the celestial equator. *Monoceros* is Greek for "unicorn." Antilocaprids were real, horned mammals related to giraffes, and the only existing one today is the North American pronghorn. The pronghorn has two horns.

2 **Fact.** The skeleton had no hindquarters and was missing part of its spine. Still, spectators flocked to the ridiculous-looking thing. Modern analysis revealed the skeleton to be a combination of mammoth and rhinoceros bones.

3 **Fact.** The "unicorn bull" existed but was not a product of nature. Dr. W. Franklin Dove of the University of Maine actually used surgery to produce the unicorn effect. When the bull was a calf, Dove removed the two horn buds and replaced them in the center of the skull. As the horns grew, they fused together, making a single large, straight horn. The spear on the bull's head was a very effective weapon, and the other bulls quickly learned not to challenge the unicorn. As a result of being secure in his power, the bull developed a very gentle manner.

"FACTS":
The Squirrel!

1 The Himalayan mole, the Florida water rat, and the pygmy beaver are not moles, rats, or beavers at all: They are each a species of squirrel.

2 A flying squirrel doesn't in fact fly, but rather glides from tree to tree. It does so with help from its *patagium*, a furry membrane that stretches between its limbs to form a kind of wing. It can also use its tail as an airfoil, increasing drag when it needs to brake and land on a tree branch.

3 While most squirrels are known for eating seeds and nuts, the thirteen-lined ground squirrel, native to North America, is much more vicious: In addition to seeds and nuts, it is known to eat insects, birds, mice, snakes, and even other thirteen-lined ground squirrels.

1 Bullsh*t!

The Himalayan mole is a mole, the Florida water rat is a muskrat, and the pygmy beaver does not exist. But believe it or not, the chipmunk, the marmot, and the prairie dog are all squirrels.

2 **Fact.** Flying squirrels have been recorded gliding as far as 295 feet! Another fitting name for flying squirrels is "bird food," since they are heavily preyed upon by nocturnal owls.

3 **Fact.** Thirteen-lined ground squirrels are omnivorous, and around 50 percent of their diet is meat. As the name suggests, these squirrels have thirteen alternating brown and white lines running the length of their bodies. They are also sometimes known as the "leopard squirrel," the "striped gopher," or the "squinny."

CHAPTER TWO

Pop Culture

"FACTS":
Albert Einstein!

1 As a child, Albert Einstein was a notoriously inconsistent (and often downright bad) student, routinely receiving low grades, particularly in math.

2 In 1930, Einstein and his student Leo Szilard patented the Einstein refrigerator, which required no electricity and had no moving parts. Despite the breakthrough innovations involved, the Einstein refrigerator never caught on.

3 Albert Einstein's face was a key inspiration for the facial design of both E.T. and Yoda. A photograph of Einstein's face sold at auction in 2017 for $125,000.

$$E = MC^2$$

1 Bullsh*t!

The persistent rumor that Einstein was a bad student is completely false. He did have brushes with authority a couple of times, but he was a brilliant student with top marks (including math). He even penned scientific papers while still a teenager and was considered to be a wunderkind.

2 Fact. Einstein was dismayed to hear of a spate of accidental deaths caused by broken refrigerator seals, which could leak harmful chemicals into the home. His design with Szilard had no moving parts, which meant no seals to break. The refrigerator did not require electricity but, instead, a heat source (such as a gas burner). Unfortunately for Einstein, conventional refrigerators were becoming more and more efficient, and they remained the norm. Modern-day engineers have revived Einstein's design, however, because it is remarkably environmentally friendly.

3 Fact. The design for the face of the iconic alien from Steven Spielberg's *E.T. the Extra-Terrestrial* was inspired by images of Carl Sandburg, Ernest Hemingway, and Albert Einstein. The face for Yoda from Star Wars was initially modeled on makeup artist Stuart Freeborn's, and features from Einstein's face were eventually incorporated, most notably his eyes and eye wrinkles, in the effort to help Yoda appear wise. The $125,000 photograph was the iconic image of Einstein sticking out his tongue. It's the most expensive photograph of the scientist ever sold.

"FACTS":
Rubik's Cube!

1 A classic Rubik's Cube has 43,252,003,274,489,856,000 possible starting positions. If you had a Rubik's Cube for every possible permutation, you could cover the surface of 30,000 earths.

2 The Rubik's Cube was first invented by naval engineer Richard James in the 1940s, who first called it "The Rubric Cube." His two sons couldn't pronounce it, calling it "Rubik's Cube" instead, and the new name stuck.

3 A Saturday-morning cartoon called *Rubik, the Amazing Cube* ran for one season in 1983. The show centered on three siblings, Carlos, Lisa, and Reynaldo Rodriguez, and their magical talking cube named Rubik. The theme song was recorded by the boy band Menudo.

1 **Fact.** When the toys first went on sale, promotional materials stated that there were "more than 3 billion" possible arrangements of a Rubik's Cube. This was correct, since there are more than 43 quintillion arrangements, but it's a gross understatement—it's even more extreme than saying the earth is home to more than one person. If you counted the permutations of the Rubik's Cube at a rate of one per second, it would take you even longer than the total age of the universe. Much longer. Despite the ridiculously high number of combinations, a team of mathematicians proved in 2010 that you are never more than twenty moves away from solving a Rubik's Cube.

2 # Bullsh*t!

Richard James, a naval engineer, did invent one of the most popular toys of all time in the 1940s: the Slinky. The Rubik's Cube was invented in 1974 by a Hungarian architect named Erno Rubik.

3 **Fact.** Rubik looked a lot like a Smurf trapped in a Rubik's Cube toy. He had all kinds of magical powers and routinely saved Carlos, Lisa, and Reynaldo from an evil magician. Before Rubik could unleash his magical powers, he had to be solved. Episodes include "Honolulu Rubik," "Back Packin' Rubik," and "Rubik and the Pooch Nappers."

"FACTS":
The Beatles!

1 Before joining the Beatles, Ringo Starr played in a very short-lived band called Beatcomber, alongside Roy Dyke, Richie Snare, Billy Shears, and Richard Starkey.

2 There was a fifth Beatle, Stuart Sutcliffe, who tragically died of an aneurysm at age twenty-one in 1962. In the same year, the Beatles' original drummer, Pete Best, was replaced by Ringo Starr.

3 The original name for the song "Hey Jude" was "Hey Jules" and was about Julian Lennon, John's son. In 1996, Julian anonymously bid £25,000 at an auction to get the original recording notes for the song.

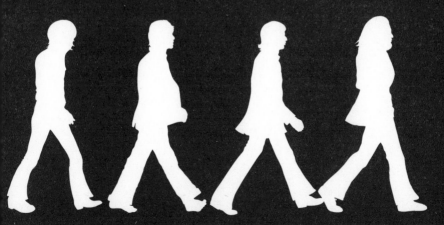

Bullsh*t!

"Beatcomber" was an alias used by John Lennon on a couple of occasions. "Roy Dyke," "Richie Snare," and "Billy Shears" are all aliases once used by Ringo Starr. "Ringo Starr" itself is a stage name; the Beatle's real name is Richard Starkey.

2 **Fact.** Sutcliffe was the band's bassist who quit in 1961 to pursue his visual art career. Some believe that his aneurysm in 1962 was a result of an earlier bar fight he had gotten into alongside John Lennon in 1961. The true cause is not known. Pete Best was the drummer for the Beatles from August 1960 to August 1962.

3 **Fact.** Paul McCartney wrote the song for Julian shortly after John split up with Julian's mother, Cynthia, in hopes that it would help him cope. McCartney later changed the name in the song to "Jude" because it "sounded better." Julian Lennon was famously bitter toward his father for years, but in the '90s, he started to acquire mementos (such as the "Hey Jude" recording notes) and publicly started to embrace his connection to John.

"FACTS":
Jeans!

1 In 1909, Solomon Levi and William Strauss patented an amazing new kind of fabric—denim—and began selling blue jeans under the company name Levi Strauss. Andrew Strauss, the great-grandson of William, is the current CEO.

2 For a long time in the US, jeans were more popularly called dungarees, a name derived from Dungri, India, where a denim-like material was made. In Danish they are called *cowboybukser* and in Hungarian, *farmernadrág*.

3 After President Barack Obama threw the first pitch at the 2009 All-Star Game in a pair of ill-fitting Levi's, he was derided by the press for wearing "dad jeans." Obama responded to the outcry, saying, "Those jeans are comfortable. And for those of you who want your president to look great in his tight jeans, I'm sorry. I'm not the guy."

1 Bullsh*t!

The company was founded as a dry goods purveyor in 1853 by Levi Strauss, a Bavarian immigrant to the United States. He did not invent denim—it had been around for hundreds of years already. Charles V. Bergh is the CEO of Levi Strauss & Co., not Andrew Strauss (a British cricket player). You generally can't patent a fabric, and it's even hard to obtain a patent on a style of clothing. Levi Strauss and his partner Jacob Davis did get a patent in 1873 for an "Improvement in Fastening Pocket-Openings," which was the method of using little copper rivets to reinforce work pants—a feature we still have on our jeans today. It is generally accepted that Levi Strauss & Co. was the first American company making and selling blue jeans.

2 **Fact.** Dungri (sometimes *Dongri*) is part of Mumbai in India, and coarse calico (similar to denim but not the same) was made there for a long time, as were pants of the material. Apparently, Danes associate jeans with cowboys, while Hungarians associate them with farmers.

3 **Fact.** Obama went on to say, "Michelle—she looks fabulous. I'm a little frumpy." Critics complained that the pants were too baggy and high-waisted and that the legs were too short.

"FACTS":
Star Wars!

1 The original Star Wars trilogy earned a combined six Oscars and ten nominations, while the subsequent trilogy received three nominations and not a single Oscar. Still, the Star Wars franchise is the highest-grossing film series of all time.

2 When Darth Vader's iconic mask was first designed, it was only supposed to appear in one small scene in the initial film.

3 In Britain's 2001 census, 390,000 people listed "Jedi" as their religious affiliation. Inspired by this, the Church of Jediism was founded in 2008 as a legitimate religion for practitioners of "the Force." A British man narrowly avoided jail after donning a trash bag, yelling "Darth Vader!", and assaulting the leader of the church with a metal crutch.

1 Bullsh*t!

The original Star Wars trilogy did not win a single Oscar, though it received six nominations. The second trilogy received twenty nominations for the Oscars, and the third trilogy received twelve nominations. Star Wars is the second-highest grossing film series of all time, after the Marvel Cinematic Universe.

2 **Fact.** Originally, Vader was supposed to be a tall, grim-faced general. Since a scene involved him crossing through the vacuum of space to board a ship, a breathing apparatus was needed. Concept artist Ralph McQuarrie designed the helmet for the one scene. Little did he know that it would become an enduring cultural icon.

3 **Fact.** Although the 390,000 census respondents were making a collective joke, the Church of Jediism is very real. To date, they have thousands of official members of the church. The founder, Barney Jones, did take a mighty thwack to the head from a crutch. His attacker, Arwel Hughes, claimed to not remember the assault because he had drunk 2 gallons of boxed wine.

"FACTS":
Star Trek!

1 In the Star Trek franchise, aliens known as the "Klingons" periodically speak Klingon, which is a grammatically complete, artificially constructed international auxiliary language created by linguist L.L. Zamenhof. Notable writers Baldur Ragnarsson, Marjorie Boulton, and Raymond Schwartz have all penned poetry in Klingon, and the horror movie *Incubus* was produced entirely in Klingon.

2 After playing Lieutenant Uhura on the first season of the original Star Trek series, Nichelle Nichols was seriously considering quitting the show. She was convinced to stay by Dr. Martin Luther King Jr., who told her she was an invaluable role model for Black women in America.

3 You could live on Star Trek Drive in either Birmingham, Alabama, or Shingletown, California; Star Trek Lane in Garland, Texas; Klingon Court in Sacramento, California; or Roddenberry Avenue (Star Trek was created by Gene Roddenberry) in Enterprise, Nevada.

1 Bullsh*t!

Most of those statements are true about a different language, Esperanto. Klingon is not an international auxiliary language because it was not designed to facilitate communication between people who have different native languages. Esperanto was designed for this purpose, as were the Universalglot, Solresol, and Volapük languages. Klingon is popular in its own right, however: A 2010 production of Charles Dickens's *A Christmas Carol* was performed entirely in Klingon; the heavy metal band Stovokor performs entirely in Klingon; and the opera 'u' was written and performed entirely in Klingon. You can even Google in Klingon.

2 **Fact.** The fact that Nichols, an African American, played a major role in a 1966 TV show was not insignificant. Nichols recalled her encounter with King: "He said, 'You have the first non-stereotypical role in television. It's not a maid's role, it's not a menial role.... This is something that is the reason we are walking, we are marching.'" Uhura's kiss with Captain Kirk in a 1968 episode is popularly regarded as the first scripted interracial TV kiss. Nichols would go on to be recruited by NASA to help encourage women and People of Color to become astronauts.

3 **Fact.** You can find them all on Google Maps. Clearly, some urban planners are fans.

"FACTS":
Helen Keller!

1 Contrary to the stories about her, Helen Keller was not born both deaf and blind.

2 Despite her blindness and deafness, Helen Keller wrote two books in her lifetime, both autobiographies: *On Your Own* and *The Secret of Inner Strength: My Story*.

3 Helen Keller was a Tuscumbian, a Wobbly, and a Swedenborgian.

1 **Fact.** Helen Keller was born on June 27, 1880, with both vision and hearing. She lost both at around eighteen months of age after an infection.

2 # Bullsh*t!

Helen Keller wrote at least twelve books during her lifetime and numerous published letters and articles. Two of her autobiographies were *The Story of My Life* and *Light in My Darkness*. *On Your Own* and *The Secret of Inner Strength: My Story* are the autobiographies of Brooke Shields and Chuck Norris, respectively.

3 **Fact.** Keller was born in Tuscumbia, Alabama, which makes her a Tuscumbian. She was a proud member of the Industrial Workers of the World union, which is also known as the "Wobblies." Finally, Keller was a member of what is now known as the "New Church," founded by Emanuel Swedenborg. Swedenborg was a mystic who believed he was appointed by God to create a new version of Christianity. Keller's book, *Light in My Darkness*, was filled with Swedenborgian philosophy.

ACTS":
etris!

Tetris was first invented in 1984 by Alexey Pajitnov, a computer programmer at the Academy of Sciences of the Soviet Union in Moscow. An early release of the game was called *TETЯIS: The Soviet Mind Game.*

Tetris is the most popular video game of all time, having sold as many as 520 million units in its various forms.

A 2009 study by the Mind Research Network, hoping to prove that playing *Tetris* was beneficial, actually discovered that playing the game repetitively is harmful to the brain's development process.

1 **Fact.** Perhaps there is a secret Communist message in *Tetris*.

2 **Fact.** From 2005 to 2011 alone, more than 100 million *Tetris* downloads were sold just for mobile phones. For reference, the original *Super Mario Bros.* for the Nintendo Entertainment System was one of the most popular games ever and sold around 40 million copies. *Tetris* debuted a year before *Super Mario Bros.* *Tetris* is the only game to be released on nearly every video game platform in existence and can even be played on some non-video-game systems, including calculators, smartphones, and *oscilloscopes*.

3 # Bullsh*t!

Not only did the Mind Research Network study prove that playing *Tetris* on a regular basis improved brain function, but the nonprofit was also alarmed to discover that playing *Tetris* regularly can make your brain bigger. The study, conducted entirely on adolescent girls, showed markedly improved brain efficiency in the regions of the brain associated with critical thinking, reasoning, and language after three months of regularly playing *Tetris*. The girls also developed noticeably thicker cortexes in two regions of the brain—the parts associated with multisensory integration and planning complex movements. As a result of the evidence, some researchers believe that playing *Tetris* could also help aging and elderly brains by slowing down deterioration.

"FACTS":
Zombies!

1 Our modern conception of zombies as shambling, flesh-eating creatures is almost entirely due to George A. Romero's seminal 1968 movie *Night of the Living Dead*. However, the word "zombie" never appears in the film.

2 *Zombies Ate My Neighbors*, *Dead Head Fred*, *Zombie Panic in Wonderland*, *Voodoo Kid*, and *Little Red Riding Hood's Zombie BBQ* are all zombie movies that came out in 1987.

3 An *actual* "zombie" named Clairvius Narcisse wandered, glassy-eyed, back into his native Haitian village in 1980 even though he had been pronounced dead in 1962. He was recognized by many relatives and acquaintances who had attended his funeral and witnessed his burial.

1 **Fact.** Before *Night of the Living Dead*, zombies were typically portrayed in popular media as living people enslaved by witch doctors. Romero's vision of the malevolent walking dead laid the foundation for most renditions of zombies we see today. The word "zombie" is not in the film at all. The creatures are referred to as ghouls.

2 # Bullsh*t!

All of those are zombie video games. The year 1987 was still good for zombie movies, however: *I Was a Teenage Zombie*, *Zombie Vs. Ninja*, *Night of the Living Babes*, *Zombie High*, *Revenge of the Living Dead Girls*, and *The Video Dead* are all examples of zombie films that came out that year.

3 **Fact.** The word "zombie" is borrowed from West Africa or Haiti (or both) and can mean either the walking dead or a person in an entranced state. The story of the Haitian zombie Clairvius Narcisse was heavily investigated by Harvard-trained anthropologist and ethnobotanist Wade Davis in the '80s, resulting in his book *The Serpent and the Rainbow*. Davis's explanation was that, in Haiti, zombies are real. The catch is that they aren't actually dead. He believes that witch doctors produced zombies by dosing victims with tetrodotoxin, the same poison found in puffer fish. The victims fall into a death-like coma and are subsequently buried alive. The witch doctor returns to the graveyard within hours, before the victim asphyxiates, and digs him up. The victim is then dosed with a powerful hallucinogen called datura, which can cause delirium, mydriasis (severe pupil dilation—that "dead" look), bizarre behavior, and amnesia.

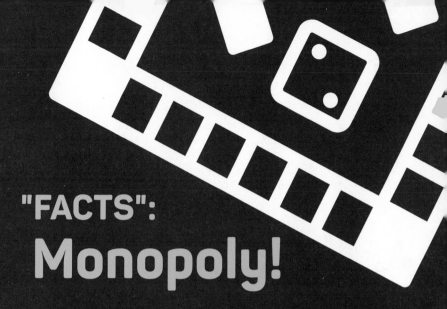

"FACTS":
Monopoly!

1 The game Monopoly is descended from a 1903 game called The Landlord's Game. The creator of the game, Lizzie Magie, intended to use the game to demonstrate that monopolies are bad for society.

2 A Monopoly game comes with $16,280 in Monopoly money. In 1965, a group of fraternity brothers at the University of Delaware were playing a highly publicized Monopoly marathon for a fundraiser and ran out of money. They made their own Monopoly money to continue the game and were subsequently sued by Parker Brothers for copyright infringement.

3 Special editions of Monopoly were created in 1941 for World War II prisoners of war in hopes to help them escape. Inside the Monopoly game were real money, a file, a compass, and a hidden compartment with a map of the local area with safe houses marked.

1 **Fact.** Though Parker Brothers rarely acknowledges it, historians have proven that Monopoly is descended from The Landlord's Game. Lizzie Magie was a devout Georgist, which means she believed that land should not be privately owned but instead belong to all humankind. She wanted her board game to show that rent impoverished tenants and enriched landlords.

2 # Bullsh*t!

First, the game comes with $20,580 in Monopoly money. (This is the same amount as the cash prize in the Monopoly World Championship.) In 1961, a marathon game held by a group of fraternity brothers at the University of Pittsburgh was stalled when the bank ran out of money. The rules of the game stated that the bank never goes broke, and so the fraternity brothers wired Parker Brothers requesting more money. Parker Brothers sent an armored car with $1 million in Monopoly money to them so that the game could continue.

3 **Fact.** The British Secret Intelligence Service approached John Waddington Ltd. (who, at the time, was the manufacturer of Monopoly outside the United States) with the idea. The "special" edition of the game was sent to POW camps by the Red Cross, and some prisoners actually made their escape with the help of the loaded board game.

"FACTS":
Dungeons & Dragons!

1 In 2004, The Waupun Correctional Institution in Wisconsin banned inmates from playing Dungeons & Dragons on the basis that the game could lead to escape fantasies and gang activity.

2 Tiny Hut, Gentle Repose, Touch of Idiocy, Warp Wood, Glibness, and Sepia Snake Sigil are all legitimate spells that magic-using player characters can "cast" in a revised version (3.5) of the "d20 System" Dungeons & Dragons.

3 Action-movie star Vin Diesel suffered the ire of D&D fans everywhere in 2020 when he publicly referred to Dungeons & Dragons players as "losers." In response to the outcry, the buff actor issued a half-hearted apology on social media.

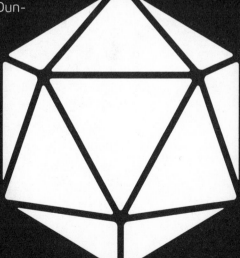

1 **Fact.** When the ban went into effect, "offending" materials were confiscated, such as miniature goblin figurines and dungeon master rule books. The ban was challenged with a lawsuit by a dedicated gamer, Kevin T. Singer, who is serving a life sentence. The lawsuit failed, and the prison's decision was upheld. In court, prison officials said they had banned Dungeons & Dragons on the advice of the prison's gang specialist and that the game could "foster an inmate's obsession with escaping from the real-life correctional environment, fostering hostility, violence, and escape behavior."

2 **Fact.** The "d20 System" is a version of Dungeons & Dragons that relies on twenty-sided dice to determine game action. In any role-playing game such as Dungeons & Dragons, players imagine the actions of their characters. While science suggests that such spells cannot be legitimately cast in real life, it is truthful to say that characters can cast them. All the spells mentioned here are listed in the rule book.

3 # Bullsh*t!

This is completely made up. Vin Diesel has been an avid Dungeons & Dragons player for over twenty years and, to this day, lights up like a giddy kid when asked about his former character "Melkor," a half-drow witch hunter. Diesel wrote the forward to the book *30 Years of Adventure: A Celebration of Dungeons & Dragons*.

"FACTS":
Martin Luther King Jr.!

1 President Reagan signed Martin Luther King Jr. Day into law in 1983, and it was first observed in 1986. Voters and lawmakers in Arizona refused to honor the holiday, which led the National Football League (NFL) to pull its plans to hold Super Bowl XXVII in Arizona in 1993.

2 Martin Luther King Jr. was posthumously given the Nobel Peace Prize in 1969 for his message of nonviolent resistance to racism, making him the first African American to earn the award.

3 The FBI tracked King extensively and wiretapped his telephone in the '50s and '60s in an attempt to prove he was a Communist. After his world-famous "I Have a Dream" speech in 1963, an FBI memo called King the "most dangerous and effective [African American] leader in the country."

1 **Fact.** Martin Luther King Jr. Day is celebrated in the US on the third Monday of every January, which falls on or near his birthday, January 15. Some conservative pundits fought hard against the holiday for a time, citing various reasons, including the idea that the holiday was just for African Americans and that the holiday was created "illegally." Arizona governor Evan Mecham railed against the holiday and did all he could to strike it down. At the time, Senator John McCain sided with Mecham. The NFL decided to move Super Bowl XXVII from the Sun Devil Stadium in Tempe, Arizona, to the Rose Bowl in Pasadena, California, after the NFL Players Association urged them to do so, costing Arizona an estimated $350 million in major convention business. Two years later, Arizona popularly voted to celebrate MLK Day. Super Bowl XXX was held at the Sun Devil Stadium.

2 # Bullsh*t!

King earned the award in 1964 while he was very much alive and was (at the time) the youngest person to ever receive the distinction. The first African American to receive the Nobel Peace Prize was Ralph Bunche, who accepted it in 1950 for his work as a mediator in Palestine.

3 **Fact.** The FBI never managed to prove any connection between King and Communism. However, the FBI did scoop up a lot of dirt about King's private life and used it in an attempt to discredit him.

"FACTS":
The Wedgie!

1 A ten-year-old boy from Grimsby, England, had to undergo emergency surgery to reattach his testicle after he received a wedgie from his classmates.

2 Residents in Salt Lake City, Utah, had to deal with the "Wedgie Bandit" from 2007 to 2009. The Bandit, later identified as Frederick Baze, would pounce on unsuspecting women in public places and yank their underwear before dashing off on foot. He was finally arrested after being caught and pinned to the ground by a local veterinary technician.

3 The Rip Away 1000 is the name of "bully-proof underwear" invented by Jared and Justin Serovich of Columbus, Ohio. As the name suggests, the underwear is designed to tear free if a malicious person yanks on it.

1 **Fact.** The English boy did not blame his friends for his injury and, in fact, admitted to the media that he himself had been in the habit of doling out wedgies. He underwent an hour-long emergency operation to reattach his testicle to the lining of his scrotum. The boys all admitted to having gotten the idea from seeing wedgies performed on *The Simpsons*.

2 # Bullsh*t!

The Wedgie Bandit doesn't exist, but a law-abiding citizen used a wedgie to good effect: When Salt Lake City thief Frederick Baze tried to steal a car, vet tech Yvonne Morris chased him and managed to stop him by giving him a wedgie. After the initial use of a wedgie, she switched to a headlock and waited for the police.

3 **Fact.** The Rip Away 1000 is real, and Jared and Justin Serovich really invented it, but the twin brothers were eight years old at the time of its invention. The Rip Away 1000 got them to the finals of a 2007 Ohio invention competition, but it didn't win first prize.

"FACTS":
LOL!

1 Expressions such as "LOL" (an acronym for "laughing out loud") have been proven to be beneficial for e-communication: A study at the University of Tasmania found that using Internet shorthand is twice as efficient for both sender and reader.

2 LOL is an airport in Nevada. Lol is a place in France. Lolol is a town in Chile. "Lol" Tolhurst was the first drummer for the English band The Cure.

3 The French equivalent of "LOL" is "MDR." Coincidentally, *lol* is a real word in both Welsh and Dutch, meaning "nonsense" and "fun," respectively.

Bullsh*t!

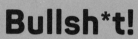

First of all, "LOL," like "ROFL," "LMAO," and "BRB," was not originally an acronym. It is an initialism and is now an acronym of sorts too. An acronym is pronounced as a word (e.g., "RADAR" or "AIDS"), and an initialism is not (e.g., "FBI" or "NAACP"). Such initialisms actually hinder communication. The University of Tasmania study found that using shorthand, such as "c u ltr b4n" ("See you later. Bye for now."), does save the sender time but takes twice as long for the receiver to understand, even if they know what it stands for.

Fact. The IATA code for Derby Field in Nevada is, in fact, LOL. The very small town of Lol is in Dordogne, France. Lolol is a town in Chile, not far from Santa Cruz. There have been several musicians who have gone by "Lol," including Laurence "Lol" Tolhurst of The Cure, the saxophonist Lol Coxhill, and the guitarist from the band 10cc, whose name is Lol Creme.

Fact. "MDR" stands for *mort de rire*, which is an expression that means "laughing" or, more literally, "died of laughter." *Lol* means "nonsense" and "fun" in Welsh and Dutch, which seems entirely appropriate.

"FACTS": Bugs Bunny!

1 Bugs Bunny got his name from a 1945 Brooklyn Heights ferryboat that several animators took on a daily basis. Brooklyn Heights had the nickname "Bugtown," often shortened to "Bugs," and the three local ferries were known colloquially as *Bugs Bunny*, *Bugs Blimpie*, and *Bugs Boxcar*.

2 From the character's inception to 1989, Bugs Bunny was voiced by Mel Blanc. Blanc was also the voice of Daffy Duck, Porky Pig, and Barney Rubble from *The Flintstones*.

3 "Mutiny on the Bunny," "Water, Water Every Hare," "Hare and Loathing in Las Vegas," "Hare-Abian Nights," and "People Are Bunny" are all real Bugs Bunny cartoons.

Bullsh*t!

That's all completely made up. Bugs Bunny got his name from Ben "Bugs" Hardaway, who was an animator and storyboard artist during animation's golden years. He drew an initial sketch of the rascally rabbit, and other members of the studio referred to it as Bugs's Bunny as it was passed around. The name stuck, and the possessive 's was eventually dropped. The first incarnation of Bugs Bunny appeared, nameless, in the cartoon *Porky's Hare Hunt* in 1938.

Fact. Known as the "man of a thousand voices," Blanc was indeed the voice of Bugs, Daffy, Porky, and Barney, not to mention Tweety Bird, Mr. Spacely (from *The Jetsons*), Captain Caveman, Speedy Gonzalez, Sylvester the Cat, Foghorn Leghorn, Yosemite Sam, Pepé Le Pew, and Wile E. Coyote.

Fact. They are, and so are "Apes of Wrath," "Hare-Way to the Stars," "Now Hare This," and "A-Lad-In His Lamp."

"FACTS":
Superman!

1 When the character of Superman was first conceived by Jerry Siegel in 1933, he was a vagrant named Bill Dunn who is given telepathic powers by a mad scientist. This Superman was an evil, bald, ruthless villain.

2 Superman in his now-ubiquitous hero form first appeared in *Action Comics #1* in 1938. The cover featured Superman lifting a car over his head. In 2023, a copy of *Action Comics #1* in fine condition sold in a private deal for $3.55 million.

3 The first feature film to star Superman was 1982's *Superman: The Movie*, starring Christopher Reeve as the Man of Steel.

1 **Fact.** Jerry Siegel first published "The Reign of the Superman," a short story about the power-hungry Dunn, which was inspired by Friedrich Nietzsche's ideas of the Übermensch, which is often translated as the "above-human," the "overman," or the "superman." The story was illustrated by Joe Shuster, and Shuster and Siegel would go on to recast Superman as the hero we know today. The villain Lex Luthor bears a lot of similarities to this original idea of Superman.

2 **Fact.** As of 2023, there were less than 100 copies of *Action Comics #1* in existence, and most of those were not in good condition. The copy in question had a quality rating of 6 out of 10, which means it was in "fine" condition. Millions of dollars might sound like a crazy price for a comic book, but some experts believe it's actually a good investment. With so few copies in existence, the value should continue to rise.

3 # Bullsh*t!

Superman: The Movie came out in 1978 and was the second feature film about Superman. The first was the black-and-white 1951 movie *Superman and the Mole Men*, which starred George Reeves as the superhero from Krypton.

"FACTS":
Supercali-
fragilistic-
expialidocious!

1 "Supercalifragilisticexpialidocious" is the longest word in the English language to appear in major dictionaries during the past several decades.

2 There were versions of the word "supercalifragilisticex-pialidocious" in popular culture before it appeared in the 1964 movie *Mary Poppins* as a song title. Gloria Parker and Barney Young wrote a song in 1951 called "Super-calafajalistickespeealadojus." The writers of the *Mary Poppins* song stated they heard a version of the word while they were boys at summer camp and that it was phrased "super-cadja-flawjalistic-espealedojus."

3 Dutch fingerstyle guitarist Eltjo Haselhoff recorded a solo acoustic guitar version of the *Mary Poppins* song "Supercalifragilisticexpialidocious" for the 2009 album *Poppin' Guitars: A Tuneful of Sherman*. The album also features the songs "Chim Chim Cher-ee," "Chitty Chitty Bang Bang," and "Let's Get Together."

Bullsh*t!

1 The word, at thirty-four letters in length, has appeared in most major dictionaries and came awfully close to being the longest. It has been beaten regularly, however, by the thirty-five-letter word "hippopotomonstrosesquipedaliophobia," which means "the fear of long words." Scientific and technical words can get very long: The forty-five-letter word "pneumonoultramicroscopic-silicovolcanoconiosis," which describes a lung condition, is the longest word to appear in major dictionaries over the last few decades.

2 **Fact.** Parker and Young actually filed a copyright-infringement suit against Wonderland Music Company, the publisher of the "Supercalifragilisticexpialidocious" song from *Mary Poppins*, but they were not success-ful. The judge ruled in favor of Wonderland because it was proven in court that many variants of the word were known prior to either song's publication. Broth-ers Richard and Robert Sherman, who wrote the song for the Disney movie, stated that they learned a ver-sion of the word while at summer camp in the Adiron-dacks in the 1930s.

3 **Fact.** Eltjo Haselhoff was one of several artists who recorded songs for the album. Australian guitarist Nick Charles recorded "Chim Chim Cher-ee," also from *Mary Poppins*. Mark Hanson recorded "Chitty Chitty Bang Bang" from the movie *Chitty Chitty Bang Bang*, and *Prai-rie Home Companion* guitarist Pat Donohue recorded "Let's Get Together" from the original *The Parent Trap*.

"FACTS": Jazz!

1 The word "jazz" comes from the Swahili word *juzi*, which means "dream."

2 Jazz historians generally agree that the first jazz record ever made was "Livery Stable Blues" from the Original Dixieland Jass Band. The record came out in 1917 and included the title song as well as "Dixie Jass Band One-Step."

3 Jelly Roll Morton, born in 1885, claimed to have invented jazz. Some of his famous jazz recordings include "Black Bottom Stomp," "Burnin' the Iceberg," "Red Hot Pepper," "Freakish," and "Creepy Feeling."

Bullsh*t!

1 The Swahili word *juzi* means "the day before yesterday," and the Swahili word for "dream" is *ndoto*. Jazz can trace its roots to the arrival of African enslaved people in the United States, but few of them would have spoken Swahili since it is from East Africa, and the American slave trade primarily preyed on West Africa. The exact etymology of the word "jazz" remains unknown. By 1912 the word was in use as slang, though not necessarily in reference to music. By 1915 the word was being used to describe Chicago music.

2 **Fact.** The 1917 single was the first major recording of music that referred to itself as jazz (or "jass," in this case) and arguably the first jazz record. Ragtime and blues, genres that are a part of jazz history but generally regarded as separate from jazz, had already been recorded extensively. The Original Dixieland Jass Band was entirely made up of white musicians.

3 **Fact.** Ferdinand Joseph LaMothe was born into a Creole community in New Orleans in 1885. During his childhood, he became a highly skilled ragtime pianist; at age fourteen, he took a job playing piano in a brothel. It was there that he took on the stage name Jelly Roll Morton, "jelly roll" being a slang term at the time for female genitalia. He was notorious for his larger-than-life persona and his frequent assertions that he invented jazz.

"FACTS":
William Shakespeare!

1 Shakespeare called his son "Hamlet" after the character from his play of the same name. Hamlet, who did not survive past infancy, was his only child.

2 "Advertising," "circumstantial," "compromise," "design," "employer," "engagement," "exposure," "investment," "luggage," "manager," "misquote," "negotiate," "pander," "petition," "reinforcement," "retirement," "swagger," "violation," "watchdog," and "worthless" are all words that were coined by Shakespeare.

3 The Globe Theatre, the famous place where Shakespeare's plays were produced, burned to the ground during the performance of one of Shakespeare's plays.

Bullsh*t!

Shakespeare had three children with his wife Anne Hathaway: Susanna, Judith, and *Hamnet*, not Hamlet. The theory goes that Shakespeare named the character after his son, not the other way around. Hamnet died of unknown causes at the age of eleven.

Fact. In some cases, Shakespeare was literally the first person to use the word, and in others, the word had a very different meaning, and he was the first to use it in the way that we use it now. Shakespeare also coined "addiction," "alligator," "bet," "bump," "critic," "downstairs," "embrace," "excitement," "eyeball," "generous," "gloomy," "glow," "grovel," "gust," "hint," "housekeeper," "hurry," "lonely," "obscene," "outbreak," "puke," "radiance," "scuffle," "shooting star," "tranquil," and "undress." There are many, many more.

Fact. The fire, which happened on June 29, 1613, started after a cannon was shot off during a scene in *Henry VIII*.

CHAPTER THREE

Everything Edible

"FACTS":
The Tomato!

1 Tomatoes are members of the genus *Solanum*, which also includes potatoes and eggplants. They are in the family Solanaceae, which includes chili peppers, tobacco, and petunias. Most of the plants in *Solanum* and Solanaceae contain parts that are poisonous to humans.

2 In the 1973 case *Nix v. Hedden*, the Supreme Court was charged with the task of determining whether the tomato was a fruit or a vegetable. It sided with the botanist, Murphy Nix, declaring the tomato to be officially a fruit.

3 The first ever genetically modified food crop to be successfully commercialized and brought to market was a biotechnology-produced tomato called the Flavr Savr.

1

Fact. The Solanaceae family is informally known as the "nightshade family." *Atropa belladonna*, or deadly nightshade, is part of the family. Plants in Solanaceae and *Solanum* are generally rich in alkaloids, which in some cases can be desirable nutritionally and in others can be downright fatal. The green parts of a tomato plant contain the alkaloid tomatine, which is toxic to humans.

2

Bullsh*t!

Nix v. Hedden did occur, although in 1893, and the Supreme Court was indeed asked to decide whether the tomato was a fruit or a vegetable. The ruling, however, was that the tomato is a vegetable. The case occurred because of a nineteenth-century law that required tax to be paid on imported vegetables but not fruit. The Supreme Court acknowledged that tomatoes are fruits in botanical terms, but decided that tomatoes are vegetables based on their typical use and popular perception.

3

Fact. Scientifically, the Flavr Savr was a success. Researchers at Calgene Inc. managed to introduce an inhibitor to tomatoes that would prevent them from producing the enzyme that causes the fruit to soften over time. The resultant Flavr Savr tomatoes stayed firm for much longer and were available in supermarkets in the US in the early '90s. Commercially, Flavr Savrs didn't last. It seems the expense of producing them and the growing public sentiment against genetically modified foods were insurmountable hurdles.

Marshmallows!

1 Marshmallow sweets date back to ancient Egypt, where the sap of the marsh mallow plant was combined with honey and nuts to make a luxury confection. In medieval Europe, marshmallow sap was used as a cure for a sore throat.

2 When modern marshmallows were invented in France, extract from the *Althaea officinalis* plant was used to create the gooey treat. Today, none of the major United States marshmallow makers use the plant *at all* to make marshmallows.

3 When high school senior Brittany Garcia walked away with only minor injuries after being hit by a car in October 2010, doctors proclaimed that marshmallows might have saved her life. The Halloween bunny costume she wore that day was made out of thousands of the little white treats.

1 **Fact.** Those Egyptians had it right. Time to convince your history professor that you need to recreate the practice. You know, for your studies. And who are we to say that marshmallows don't cure a sore throat? Try it the next time you get the flu.

2 **Fact.** Marshmallows get their name from the marsh mallow (scientific name *Althaea officinalis*), a pink-flowered plant that, naturally, grows in marshes. There are other kinds of mallow, including musk mallow, tree mallow, and Indian mallow. Marsh mallow sap is sweet. Big-brand marshmallows that are sold in stores are made from primarily corn syrup, starch, sugar, water, and, in place of marshmallow extract, gelatin. Most people have probably never tried a "real" marshmallow.

3
Bullsh*t!

That's ridiculous. Who makes a bunny costume out of marshmallows? In reality, marshmallows kill. At least two people have died playing the game chubby bunny, which involves stuffing your mouth with as many marshmallows as possible, including a twelve-year-old girl who suffocated to death while playing the game at a school fair.

"FACTS":
Beer!

1 Beer is mostly water. Because of this, the type of water used in the beer-making process has a significant effect on the taste of the beer. Dublin's hard water is most suitable for stouts, while Pilsen's soft water is best for pale lagers.

2 According to annual Gallup polls, about 78 percent of US adults "have occasion to use alcoholic beverages." When it comes to beverage of choice, it has been nearly a dead heat between wine and beer since the mid-1940s, with wine slightly edging ahead of beer each year. Beer took the lead only once, in 2005.

3 A program was launched in Belgium in 2001 to replace sugary drinks and soda in school lunch-rooms with a healthier option: beer. Students had the option between lager and bitter, and 80 percent of the children in the pilot programs said they enjoyed having beer with lunch.

1 **Fact.** Typical ingredients of beer are water (mostly), a fermented starch, yeast, and a flavoring, such as hops. The mineral content of the water used does have an effect on the taste of the beer. Hard water, high in minerals such as calcium and sulfate, enhances bitterness. Soft water, free of most minerals, has a cleaner taste. This is likely why Guinness brewed in Dublin tastes different from Guinness brewed in London.

2 # Bullsh*t!

Actually, the reverse is true when it comes to alcoholic beverage preference. Beer has maintained the lead each year, with wine nipping at its heels. The exception is 2005, when wine took the top honors by three percentage points. Hard liquor is fairly distant in third place. We're also a little dryer than stated: Gallup reports that only 62 percent of US adults drink alcohol occasionally, and it has been that way since the mid-1940s, with a brief increase during the 1970s (up to 71 percent).

3 **Fact.** Rony Langenaeken, the chairman of De Limburgse Biervrienden, the beer club behind the plan, was quoted as saying: "Beer is for the whole family." The program was drawn out for students ages three to fifteen. A special beer was used for the pilot programs, called tafelbier, which contained no more than 2.5 percent alcohol.

"FACTS": Sliced Bread!

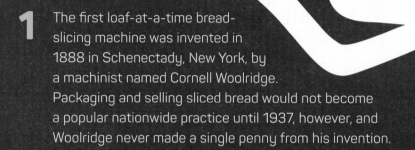

1 The first loaf-at-a-time bread-slicing machine was invented in 1888 in Schenectady, New York, by a machinist named Cornell Woolridge. Packaging and selling sliced bread would not become a popular nationwide practice until 1937, however, and Woolridge never made a single penny from his invention.

2 A bakery in Chillicothe, Missouri, was the first to sell pre-sliced bread. They called it Kleen Maid Bread and marketed it as "the greatest forward step in the baking industry since bread was wrapped." From this, the phrase "the greatest thing since sliced bread" is thought to have originated.

3 Selling sliced bread was banned by the US government in 1943 at the height of World War II. The order was given by Claude R. Wickard, the secretary of agriculture at the time. The ban was supposed to help conserve wax paper (which was needed to keep sliced bread fresh) and to bring the cost of bread down.

1 Bullsh*t!

The first loaf-at-a-time bread-slicing machine was invented in 1928 by a jeweler named Otto Rohwedder of Davenport, Iowa. It was a big hit. In 1930, the Continental Baking Company introduced pre-sliced Wonder Bread, using machines that were improved versions of Rohwedder's design. Rohwedder sold the machines for two decades before retiring.

2 **Fact.** The Chillicothe Baking Company bought Rohwedder's first automatic bread slicer in 1928 and put it to work. On July 7, 1928, a prophetic columnist wrote in the *Chillicothe Constitution-Tribune*: "So neat and precise are the slices...that one realizes instantly that here is a refinement that will receive a hearty and permanent welcome."

3 **Fact.** It turns out that most major bakeries had huge stores of wax paper already, and the ban did not decrease the price of bread. Most importantly, the ban was hugely unpopular. A letter from a frustrated homemaker appeared in *The New York Times* on January 26, 1943: "I should like to let you know how important sliced bread is to the morale and saneness of a household. My husband and four children are all in a rush during and after breakfast. Without ready-sliced bread I must do the slicing for toast—two pieces for each one—that's ten. For their lunches I must cut by hand at least twenty slices, for two sandwiches apiece. Afterward I make my own toast. Twenty-two slices of bread to be cut in a hurry!" The ban was lifted on March 8, 1943.

"FACTS":
High-Fructose Corn Syrup!

1 High-fructose corn syrup is made by soaking and fermenting corn kernels to extract cornstarch, then using enzymes to turn the glucose in the starch into fructose. It is a primary sweetener in American processed foods because it is cheaper than sugar. Many studies have suggested that high-fructose corn syrup is more harmful to the body than cane sugar.

2 The average US citizen consumes more than 40 pounds of high-fructose corn syrup each year and well over 100 pounds of sweeteners in general (including sugar).

3 In a 2011 study at Wesleyan University, trace amounts of toxic chemicals were found in samples of the high-fructose corn syrup used by major American food companies, including ammonia, formaldehyde, and acetone.

1 **Fact.** Corn syrup is cheaper in the United States thanks to long-running heavy government subsidies on corn. Add to that a stiff import tax on sugar, and it's no wonder why major food companies sweeten with syrup. The stuff also stores better, doesn't mask flavors like regular sugar, has a lower freezing point, and retains moisture well. There is still plenty of controversy as to whether there is a significant nutritional difference between high-fructose corn syrup and table sugar (which is made from sugarcane or sugar beets and is primarily sucrose), but many studies suggest that the syrup contributes to the obesity epidemic.

2 **Fact.** The United States Department of Agriculture's Economic Research Service calculates the per capita availability of sweeteners in the US by year. The numbers can't tell us *exactly* how much high-fructose corn syrup each person consumes, but they do reflect the buying habits of the consumer. Since 1985, the per capita availability has been well over 40 pounds. We may be consuming as much as 50 pounds per year of the gooey stuff and 60 pounds of sugar. And remember, that's *on average*, meaning there's a hefty squad of people out there who are consuming more.

3 # Bullsh*t!

High-fructose corn syrup may be bad for you, but it's not *that* bad. You can find those chemicals, however, in cigarettes and cigarette smoke, along with cyanide and carbon monoxide. It is true, however, that high-fructose corn syrup is sometimes made with hydrochloric acid.

"FACTS":
Bacon!

1 The bacon we typically eat in the United States is back meat from a pig that has been smoked and cured. The word "bacon" comes from the Latin *bacca*, which (appropriately) means "back."

2 In 2009, chefs and students at Lock Haven University used 225 pounds of bacon to construct a 203-foot-long BLT sandwich.

3 The American company J&D's offers bacon-flavored lip balm. The delicious balms contain bacon flavoring so you can taste bacon every time you moisturize your lips. The company also sells bacon-scented underwear.

① Bullsh*t!

Pork loin and fatback, both from the back of the pig, are popular kinds of bacon in other countries. The bacon most Americans eat comes from the underside of the pig, or pork belly. In fact, the USDA defines bacon as the "cured belly of a swine carcass." Bacon is cured (but not necessarily smoked) before a person buys it. Smoking is just one of the many glorious ways to prepare and enjoy bacon. The word "bacon" actually comes from the Old High German *bahho*, which means "bacon" or "buttock." Since bacon back then likely came from the back and buttocks of the pig, the word probably meant both! *Bacca* is a kind of fruit.

② **Fact.** The mighty sandwich, which also featured 200 pounds of tomatoes and 165 pounds of lettuce, was undertaken to beat the previous world record of 179 feet. Lock Haven students did not waste time admiring their creation: The massive BLT was consumed immediately. The record has since been beaten by a few other groups of people.

③ **Fact.** J&D's company slogan is "Everything should taste like bacon." J&D's is also popular for its Bacon Salt and its bacon-flavored mayonnaise, Baconnaise.

"FACTS":
Pepper!

1 The black pepper on the tables of your neighborhood restaurant is the ground, dried fruit of the *Piper nigrum* plant, which is a perennial flowering woody vine. The plant is native to India, but the world's largest cultivator of *Piper nigrum* is Vietnam.

2 Although it is now one of the most common spices in the world, black pepper was once so valuable that it was used as currency.

3 The Egyptian pharaoh Ramesses II used black pepper as a means of torture: On his orders, victims *had their orifices stuffed* with hundreds of little black peppercorns.

1 **Fact.** *Piper nigrum* is indeed the scientific name of the black pepper plant. Peppercorns are, scientifically, fruits. Black pepper is a perennial flowering woody vine because it lives for longer than two years, produces flowers, has stems that are made of wood, and is a climbing plant. *Piper nigrum* is native to India, but it is a major crop in Vietnam, which produces a third of the world's black pepper.

2 **Fact.** Throughout most of history, the vast majority of black pepper came from India. The spice was in great demand, and those who could control the spice trade gained a huge economic advantage. Pepper was highly coveted in ancient Greece and Rome, and in medieval Europe it was sometimes used as collateral or currency. The Dutch word *peperduur*, meaning "expensive as pepper," is still in use today. Desire for an overseas black pepper trade route to India was a major motivation for the Portuguese to conduct their sea voyages, which spawned the Age of Discovery.

3 # Bullsh*t!

It's unlikely that Ramesses II ever ordered to have someone stuffed with black pepper. However, the mummy of Ramesses II was discovered with black peppercorns in its abdomen and packed inside its nose. Egyptologists have been baffled by this, since it's an uncommon practice. One benefit Ramesses II enjoys because of his pepper-lined nose is a decent profile: Most mummies have flattened noses thanks to the wrapping process, but Ramesses II still has a distinct, hook-shaped nose.

"FACTS":
Watermelon!

1 The watermelon is the official state fruit of Oklahoma. Scientifically speaking, the watermelon is also a kind of nut.

2 The National Watermelon Association annually crowns a National Watermelon Queen. The queen is selected in a pageant "with focus on speech and interview" skills.

3 An old Romani legend from the Balkans maintained that a watermelon left alone for too long could turn into a vampire. Vampire watermelons were thought to growl, roll around, and thirst for blood.

① Bullsh*t!

In 2007, Oklahoma named the watermelon its official state vegetable. The watermelon is definitely a fruit, not a vegetable, though it is in the family Cucurbitaceae, which includes squash, pumpkin, and zucchini, all of which, scientifically, are fruits. Why does Oklahoma call the watermelon a vegetable? They already had a state fruit—the strawberry. Also, watermelons are not nuts at all. But they are, technically, berries. A berry is a fleshy fruit derived from a single ovary. Watermelons are also classified as "pepos," which are berries with hard rinds.

② Fact. The lucky lady is crowned each year at the National Watermelon Association's convention.

③ Fact. It is an actual, documented legend, although there is some debate as to whether this was a serious belief or a funny story passed down through generations in the style of fairy tales. Tatomir P. Vukanović, a Balkan historian, wrote about the legend in an article for the *Journal of the Gypsy Lore Society*: "Vampires of ground fruit origin are believed to have the same shape and appearance as the original plant....[They] go round the houses, stables, and rooms at night, all by themselves, and do harm to people. But it is thought that they cannot do great damage to folk, so people are not very afraid of this kind of vampire." So, next time you have a slice of watermelon, consider yourself a hero for preventing a vampire attack.

"FACTS":
Cheese!

1 Our seventh president, Andrew Jackson, was known for throwing White House parties that were open to the public. At his last party, President Jackson served a 3-foot-high, 4-foot-diameter, 1,400-pound wheel of cheddar, which was consumed by guests in two hours.

2 Velveeta, Easy Cheese (in a spray can), and the square American Kraft Singles are *not* cheeses and contain no real cheese at all. All three are made of soy protein concentrate.

3 A study by the British Cheese Board concluded that eating a piece of cheese before sleep produced vivid dreams. The results indicated that different types of cheese produce different types of dreams.

1 **Fact.** The enormous wheel of cheese was a gift, and Jackson reportedly let it age for two years in the White House lobby. He offered it to guests during his last party, and they consumed it immediately. Historians note that the lobby was left with numerous cheese stains and that it smelled like cheese for weeks.

2 # Bullsh*t!

Velveeta, Easy Cheese, and American Kraft Singles are all made with real cheese, but they cannot legally be called cheese because of rules dictated by the Food and Drug Administration. In truth, they are processed cheese, which is cheese that has various ingredients added, such as emulsifiers, whey, unfermented milk products (like cream), salt, and food coloring. That said, the fancy herbed Brie you find at the store has ingredients added (little green herb flecks), but the FDA doesn't require it to be labeled "pasteurized prepared cheese product."

3 **Fact.** Wacky but true. The British Cheese Board's goal for the study was to determine whether eating cheese before bed leads to nightmares, as a popular myth claims. The study's volunteers reported few nightmares, but most reported vivid dreams. Researchers noticed a link between types of dreams and the type of cheese consumed. Volunteers who ate cheddar seemed to dream about celebrities, while those who consumed Red Leicester had nostalgic dreams. Volunteers who sampled Lancashire dreamed about work, while those who ate blue cheese reported very vivid, bizarre dreams.

"FACTS":
The Sandwich!

1 The Sandwich Islands, an equatorial volcanic archipelago in the Pacific that sits 500 miles west of Ecuador, were named by British explorer Edward Teach after his patron, John Capulet, the forty-seventh Earl of Sandwich. The sandwich was invented by Capulet.

2 In 2006, a Massachusetts state senator, Jarrett Barrios, threatened legislation to restrict schools from serving Fluffernutter sandwiches more than once a week to children. The measure caused a major uproar from his constituents and even other politicians, including a state representative, Kathi-Anne Reinstein, who promised to file legislation that would make the Fluffernutter the official sandwich of Massachusetts.

3 According to a court ruling in Boston, a sandwich must include "at least two slices of bread." The court ruling went on to state that burritos, quesadillas, and tacos are therefore not sandwiches.

Bullsh*t!

The islands 500 miles west of Ecuador are not the Sandwich Islands—they are called the Galápagos Islands. The "Sandwich Islands" was the first name given to a different Pacific archipelago, which we know as Hawaii. The explorer James Cook (not Edward Teach, who was the pirate Blackbeard) named the Hawaiian Islands the Sandwich Islands after John Montagu, the fourth Earl of Sandwich. Montagu, an industrious man, used to insist on his lunch arriving between two pieces of bread so that he could continue to work. It is said that others would order their meat "the same as Sandwich!" and the term was born.

2 **Fact.** In case you were unaware, a Fluffernutter is a white-bread sandwich with a layer of peanut butter and a layer of marshmallow cream. Senator Barrios was understandably reacting to the low nutritional value of the sandwich his son Nathaniel had been given at school, but he failed to properly assess the public opinion in Massachusetts of the decadent treat. (Marshmallow Fluff was invented in Somerville, Massachusetts.) In response to the furor, Barrios abandoned his mission, and Representative Reinstein retracted hers as well.

3 **Fact.** The court made the ruling after Panera Bread filed a complaint that its no-compete clause in a shopping center was violated by the introduction of a Qdoba Mexican Eats. Since Panera produces sandwiches, and Qdoba produces burritos, the court found that there was, in fact, no competition between the restaurants.

"FACTS": Tequila!

1 A bottle of tequila sold in 1996 for $225,000, earning it the Guinness World Record for most expensive bottle of spirits ever sold. The same company was eager to break its own record, and in 2010 unveiled a bottle of tequila on sale for $3.5 million.

2 When mescal and tequila were first produced in Mexico, it was traditional for the bottle to have a worm at the bottom, which was seen as a seal of quality. Nowadays, export bottles rarely have worms in them because of negative public perception, but the worms are still very much present in true Mexican tequila.

3 Tequila is not just a drink— it's a scientific marvel. Physicists from the National Autonomous University of Mexico discovered how to make diamonds out of tequila.

1 **Fact.** Distiller Hacienda la Capilla produced the 1996 bottle, which was designed by Mexican artist Alejandro Gomez Oropeza. The bottle was made from solid platinum and white gold and was filled with Ley .925 Pasión Azteca tequila. The newest bottle, going for $3.5 million, is made of ceramic with a 5-pound layer of platinum and more than 4,000 diamonds totaling 328 carats.

2 # Bullsh*t!

It was never traditional to put a worm in a bottle of tequila or mescal. The idea to put worms in bottles of mescal was drummed up by American marketers in the 1940s. If you find a worm in your tequila, throw it away: The Norma Oficial Mexicana (Official Mexican Standard) forbids the practice of putting any invertebrate life forms into bottles of tequila. The worm in question is actually not a worm but a caterpillar—specifically, the larval form of the *Hypopta agavis* moth—which feeds on the agave plant and is considered a delicacy in parts of Mexico.

3 **Fact.** Amazingly, tequila has the precise proportion of carbon, hydrogen, and oxygen atoms necessary to create diamonds. The scientists heat eighty-proof tequila to over 1,400°F, which results in a very fine film of synthetic diamond. The resulting diamond crystals are far too thin to use for jewelry, but they are extremely hard and quite heat-resistant and are hoped to have a variety of industrial applications.

"FACTS": Chocolate!

1 In 1943, the US Army requested Hershey to make a chocolate bar ration for World War II soldiers. By the end of the war, Hershey had produced over 380 million 2-ounce Tropical Chocolate Bars, which were designed to withstand temperatures of up to 120°F without melting.

2 Chocolate is lethally poisonous to cats. We humans can enjoy chocolate to our hearts' content, but we'd better keep it far away from our pets. It can give a nasty stomachache to dogs, but it is particularly dangerous to our feline friends due to their smaller body size, and the fact that a cat's tongue has five times as many sweetness receptors as a dog's.

3 Chocolate comes from the seeds of the cacao tree, an evergreen tree native to tropical parts of the Americas. The cacao tree comes from the genus *Theobroma*, which means "food of the gods."

1 **Fact.** The chocolate bars remained exceptionally hard in extremely hot conditions; they were included in sundries kits for soldiers in the Korean War and the Vietnam War as well. Some veterans hasten to point out, however, that while the chocolate bar did not melt in your pocket, it did not readily melt in your mouth either, and that it wasn't very tasty. The Tropical Chocolate Bar also went to the moon—it was on board the Apollo 15 mission in 1971.

2 # Bullsh*t!

Chocolate is not particularly dangerous for cats. It is highly toxic to them, but they are simply not interested in it. Why? Cats cannot perceive sweetness at all. Dogs are at a high risk for chocolate poisoning. A large dog would feel the effects after eating a bar of chocolate and could die after eating several of them. Chocolate is poisonous to humans too. You would have to consume many pounds of chocolate to feel the effects, but people still manage to poison themselves with it on a regular basis. The toxic culprit is the alkaloid theobromine, which is particularly present in dark chocolate and baker's chocolate.

3 **Fact.** The evergreen cacao tree (*Theobroma cacao*) is native to tropical regions of the Americas, particularly Central America. The tree produces large fruit pods, which are full of cocoa beans (this plant's seeds). *Theobroma* comes from the Greek *theos*, meaning "god," and the Greek *bromos*, which means "food," and more specifically, "oats." Technically, you could say chocolate is the "oat of the gods."

"FACTS":
The Hot Dog!

1 According to the American Hot Dog Society, about 2 billion hot dogs are consumed in the US each year.

2 The name "hot dog" has its roots in the nineteenth century, when many street sausage vendors were believed to actually serve dog meat. By 1843, newspaper editors were referring to "dog-meat sausages" and "dog sandwiches."

3 *Hot Dog* was the name of a Saturday morning children's documentary show starring Jonathan Winters, Jo Anne Worley, and Woody Allen. One introduction to the show included Woody Allen looking into the camera and saying, "*Hot Dog*. A program about stuff."

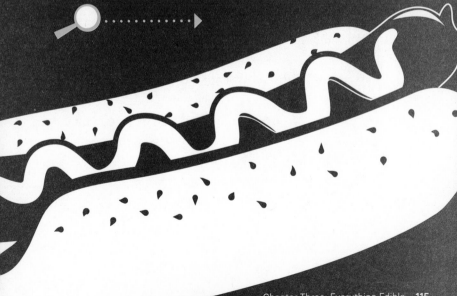

1 Bullsh*t!

As far as we know, there is no American Hot Dog Society—yet. But the venerated National Hot Dog & Sausage Council asserts that we eat 20 billion hot dogs in this country each year. The length of that many hot dogs is nearly enough to go to the moon and back four times.

2 **Fact.** Whether the crafty street vendors actually served dog or not is something best left to the shrouded mists of history. The dog-meat rumor, however, persisted throughout most of the nineteenth century. In the mid-1890s, it seems the slang "hot dog" was in regular use on college campuses. By 1896, both Yale and Harvard had multiple references to hot dogs in their publications, including humorous allusions to the rumor of the sausages' dubious canine provenance.

3 **Fact.** *Hot Dog* only aired for one season on NBC, from 1970 to 1971, and was later syndicated in reruns, also for one year, from 1977 to 1978. The pilot episode featured Allen, Worley, and Tom Smothers (of the Smothers Brothers). Winters replaced Smothers when the show was picked up. Each show was dedicated to answering kids' questions about everyday objects. Most of the music for the show was recorded by the Youngbloods. *Hot Dog* was the only TV series—aside from a miniseries called *Crisis in Six Scenes*—in which Woody Allen appeared regularly.

"FACTS":
The Ice Cream Sundae!

1 Five American cities claim to be the birthplace of the ice cream sundae: Ithaca, New York; Evanston, Illinois; Cleveland, Ohio; Buffalo, New York; and Two Rivers, Wisconsin. In its early days the sundae was spelled multiple ways, including "sunday," "sondie," "sundi," "sundhi," and "sundaye."

2 Despite its American origin, South Koreans are huge fans of the ice cream sundae, which is a popular street food throughout the country. The Korean version is even sweeter and richer than the original.

3 New York City's Serendipity 3 restaurant features a $1,000 sundae on its menu.

1 **Fact.** Each of the five cities has evidence for its claim, but none have conclusive proof. Maybe the ice cream sundae was such a good idea that it was invented in five places at once. Evanston's story is particularly charming: In the late nineteenth century, religious leaders enacted a law prohibiting the sale of ice cream sodas on Sundays. The story goes that drug store owners started serving ice cream with syrup instead of soda, and thus obeyed the letter of the law, if not the spirit. The confection became known as the "Sunday," and later the appellation "sundae," so as not to further enrage the devout. In the end, nobody is sure who actually invented the sundae!

2 # Bullsh*t!

Koreans do love *sundae* very much, and it is a popular street food in South Korea. But Korean *sundae* is nothing like the ice cream sundae. *Sundae* is a traditional blood sausage made by stuffing intestines with noodles and pig's blood.

3 **Fact.** Serendipity 3 does offer a $1,000 Golden Opulence Sundae, which is covered with edible 23-karat gold leaf, Amedei Porcelana chocolate, and rare candies. It's served in a crystal goblet, with a side of passion-fruit-infused Grand Passion Caviar. According to the owners, Serendipity 3 sells an average of one Golden Opulence Sundae per month, and you must order it in advance.

"FACTS":
The Apple!

1 Nearly every kind of apple we eat today is descended from one species, *Malus sieversii*, a wild apple that still grows in the Ili Valley of Kazakhstan. The wild apples of *Malus sieversii* are some of the largest apples available today, and the plant is especially hardy, but it is nevertheless threatened by extinction.

2 The Granny Smith apple is named after Maria Ann Smith, a nineteenth-century farmer. She produced the apple in her Australian orchard by accident.

3 In the book of Genesis, the serpent tempts Eve with an apple, the forbidden fruit from the tree of knowledge. The Norse goddess Sjöfn was said to have been poisoned by an apple and cursed to eternally roam the underworld, giving apples to the dead. The Greek god Dionysus was often associated with apples and commonly depicted as eating or holding an apple.

1 **Fact.** *Malus sieversii* apples are big and colorful, and the tree is capable of growing and producing fruit in harsher conditions than most domestic varieties. It still grows wild in the Ili Valley in Kazakhstan (which stretches into border regions of China), but scientists and cultivators have begun to plant and study the wild apple in hopes of gaining insight into growing and breeding better apples. The apple you had for lunch is *Malus domestica*.

2 **Fact.** "Granny" Smith cultivated many kinds of apples, and the Granny Smith variety emerged quite accidentally as a hybrid of two different species. The apples became popular locally, winning competitions, and neighboring orchards began to acquire the seedlings and produce Granny Smiths themselves. Today, there are more than 7,500 cultivars of apple.

3 # Bullsh*t!

The serpent does tempt Eve with a forbidden fruit in the book of Genesis, but nowhere is it identified as an apple. In fact, numerous religious scholars have suggested other fruits, like the grape, fig, tamarind, or pomegranate. The apple often appears in Western artistic depictions of the story; one theory is that the choice originated as a pun because the Latin word for apple is identical to the word for evil (*malum*). The Norse goddess Sjöfn was associated with love, whereas Iðunn was the goddess of apples and youth. Apples were associated with fertility and youthfulness. Additionally, Dionysus, the Greek god of the harvest, wine, and ecstasy, was commonly depicted with grapes.

"FACTS":
The Fortune Cookie!

1 Fortune cookies are not Chinese in origin at all. Amazingly, fortune cookies are from Japan. They stem from the tradition of *omikuji*, which are fortunes written on little slips of paper and given out at Shinto shrines and Buddhist temples.

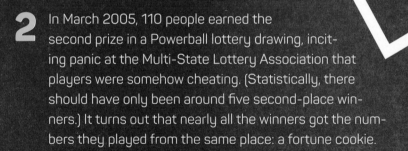

2 In March 2005, 110 people earned the second prize in a Powerball lottery drawing, inciting panic at the Multi-State Lottery Association that players were somehow cheating. (Statistically, there should have only been around five second-place winners.) It turns out that nearly all the winners got the numbers they played from the same place: a fortune cookie.

3 Currently, around 800 million fortune cookies are made for export each year in China.

1 **Fact.** Fortune cookies have never been Chinese, and you won't find them in China now. In fact, a recent attempt to market fortune cookies to the Chinese was met with failure—they are "too American." Records dating back to the eighteenth century show Japanese people making a version of the fortune cookie, and the practice probably began long before that. It is still unclear precisely how the practice was adopted by Chinese restaurateurs in the US. One theory is that the original Japanese fortune-cookie makers might have been detained during the Japanese-American internment in 1942, leaving a niche that Chinese workers filled.

2 **Fact.** The Multi-State Lottery Association had to distribute $19 million in unexpected payouts after winners got their numbers from fortune cookies that were manufactured by Wonton Food in Long Island City, New York. Wonton Food pumps out 4 million fortune cookies a day in their factory and supplies them to restaurants all over the country. When told by *The New York Times* that 110 people had won the lottery thanks to their fortune cookies, Wonton Food vice president of sales Derrick Wong said, "That's very nice!"

3 # Bullsh*t!

Fortune cookies are a distinctively American industry. The vast majority of the 3 billion made each year are produced here in the US.

"FACTS":
Honey!

1 Honey is an ancient food. Humans have collected and eaten honey for well over 10,000 years. Honey was cultivated in ancient China and Mesoamerica, and it was a popular sweetener in ancient Egypt. The Egyptians and Assyrians sometimes used honey to embalm the dead.

2 Honey is flower nectar that has been consumed and subsequently excreted by honeybees. The nectar is consumed, pooped, consumed again, and pooped thousands of times before it adopts the viscous consistency and amber color that we like in our honey.

3 It's possible to become severely intoxicated by eating honey. Honey made from certain rhododendrons contains grayanotoxin—eating it can make you dizzy, weak, and nauseated, and can cause you to sweat and vomit. Toxic honey was used (with lethal effect) as a weapon against the Roman forces of Pompey during his campaign in Asia Minor.

1 **Fact.** In Spain, a cave painting more than 10,000 years old depicts women gathering honey. In ancient times, Mayans cultivated honeybees, which they regarded as sacred. Beekeeping was practiced in China 3,000 years ago. Even without refrigeration, honey in a properly sealed container can last indefinitely. In ancient Egypt and parts of the Middle East, corpses were sometimes embalmed in honey. It's nice to know that some mummies are sweet on the inside.

2 # Bullsh*t!

Honey is not bee poop. Bee vomit would be a more apt description but still not strictly correct. Dehydrated bee regurgitation is pretty spot-on. In the hive, the nectar is regurgitated mouth to mouth from one bee to another until it is deposited in the wax honeycomb. Thousands of bees help to dry out the nectar by flapping their wings. (This is why a beehive is constantly buzzing.) The result is the gloppy goo that we love so much.

3 **Fact.** In the first century B.C.E., the Roman legions passed through a narrow valley and came across a large cache of honey. As pillaging soldiers are wont to do, they appropriated the sweet stuff and consumed it on the spot. Little did they know the toxic honey was a gift from their enemies. As the legions fell collectively sick, they were ambushed and easily slaughtered. In mild cases of toxic honey, you're back to normal in twenty-four hours. In extreme cases, toxic honey can kill.

"FACTS":
Gummy Bears!

1 The gummy bear was invented in 1922 by Hans Riegel Sr. in Bonn, Germany. It was originally called the Dancing Bear, which he delivered personally to customers on his bicycle. The company he founded is still around today and is still a major international seller of gummy bears.

2 Gummy bears and other gummy candies contain the gelatin-friendly sweetener xylitol, which has been found to be three times as likely to cause cavities and tooth decay compared to regular sugar.

3 A North Carolina company makes and sells the World's Largest Gummy Bears. The behemoths are larger than a football, weighing in at 5 pounds and measuring 9 inches tall. One giant gummy bear has 12,600 calories, representing the equivalent of 1,400 regular-sized gummy bears.

1 **Fact.** Hans Riegel Sr. founded the Haribo company in 1920 (Hans + Riegel + Bonn = Haribo). Haribo gummy bears are ubiquitous and popular, and they are sold worldwide as Goldbears Gummi Candy.

2 # Bullsh*t!

The gummy bears we buy in stores do not contain xylitol and are no more likely to cause cavities than any other candy. Recent scientific studies have tried out gummy bears with xylitol in them on children and found that not only are xylitol-laced gummy bears less likely to cause cavities, but that the sweetener actually fights cavities and prevents tooth decay. However, keep in mind that this sweetener is highly toxic to dogs!

3 **Fact.** It is not known if they truly are the world's largest gummy bears, but that is the official name of the product manufactured by GGB Candies of Raleigh. One bear has a shelf life of about a year, which is about how long you'll need to eat all ninety servings.

"FACTS":
The Twinkie!

1 In 2010, as an example for his students, a nutrition professor at Kansas State University went on a "Twinkie diet" for eight weeks, eating only junk food items from a convenience store at every meal. The result? He gained a whopping 27 pounds.

2 Former President Clinton is a fan of the Twinkie. He placed one inside his National Millennium Time Capsule, alongside the complete literary works of William Faulkner and the recordings of Louis Armstrong.

3 The urban legend that claims Twinkies have a shelf life of over ten years is patently false. A Twinkie does last longer than most baked goods, but its actual shelf life won't blow any minds: twenty-six days.

Bullsh*t!

The "Twinkie diet" lasted ten weeks, and Professor Mark Haub lost 27 pounds. The trick? Calorie counting. By limiting himself to 1,800 calories a day, the professor reached his ideal weight, his bad cholesterol went down, and his good cholesterol went up. Haub ate Twinkies every day on the diet, as well as Nutty Buddy bars, powdered donuts, and Doritos.

2 **Fact.** Clinton's time capsule was to be filled with artifacts, ideas, and accomplishments that represented America at the turn of the millennium. Besides Faulkner, Armstrong, and the Twinkie, future people will find a model of the Liberty Bell, the Hawaiian state flag, a picture of US soldiers liberating a concentration camp, and children's artwork.

3 **Fact.** One urban legend asserts that Twinkies have a shelf life of forever, which is, of course, impossible. Twenty-six days is a long time for even a snack cake to last, but Twinkies are capable of this because they lack dairy ingredients.

"FACTS":
Spam!

1 In 2005, a limited-edition flavor of Spam was issued by Hormel: Spam Golden Honey Grail. The collector's edition tin (and the sweet, sweet meat inside) was timed to coincide with the production of the Broadway musical *Monty Python's Spamalot*.

2 While jokesters will tell you that Spam stands for "something posing as meat," the name was created in 1941 as a short form of "supply-pressed ham."

3 Spam was a major staple during World War II for Allied soldiers. Soviet leader Nikita Khrushchev said, "Without Spam, we wouldn't have been able to feed our army." President Eisenhower said, "I ate my share of Spam, along with millions of other soldiers."

1 **Fact.** In a perfect example of "if you can't beat 'em, join 'em," Hormel got in on the fun with the coveted cans of honey-drenched mystery meat. Original Monty Python member and writer of the musical Eric Idle said, "Spam is the holy grail of canned meats!"

2 # Bullsh*t!

When the product was first launched, it was boringly called Hormel Spiced Ham. Hormel held a contest in 1937 to come up with a more exciting name. An actor named Kenneth Daigneau came up with Spam, short for "spiced ham," and earned the $100 prize money.

3 **Fact.** During the war, Hormel shipped 15 million cans a week to Allied soldiers. Khrushchev's remark comes from his autobiography and Eisenhower's from a 1966 letter to the then-head of Hormel, H.H. Corey. Eisenhower went on to write, "I'll even confess to a few unkind remarks about it—uttered during the strain of battle, you understand. But as former commander in chief, I believe I can still officially forgive you your only sin: sending so much of it!"

CHAPTER FOUR

Weird
Science

"FACTS":
The Sun!

1   The sun is a class GV star, which is also known as a "yellow dwarf." The term is a misnomer because the sun is, in fact, *not* yellow but white. While it may be a dwarf compared to giant stars, the sun and other yellow dwarfs outshine 90 percent of the stars in our galaxy.

2   The sun is not only moving—it's also very fast. It is currently traveling hundreds of miles per second through an area called the Local Bubble.

3   Hear that ticking? The sun is actually a time bomb of a sort—it is contracting and cooling down and will eventually undergo a gravitational collapse, exploding into a supernova, which will destroy Earth. But don't panic. We have 10 billion years to prepare for our fate.

1 **Fact.** The sun is, in fact, white and only appears yellow to us due to atmospheric scattering of blue light. Most of the stars in our galaxy are red dwarfs, which are not nearly as bright as the sun.

2 **Fact.** Our planet orbits the sun, and the sun orbits the center of the Milky Way. While Earth takes roughly 365 days to orbit the sun, it takes the sun roughly 250 million years to complete its orbit. The sun is traveling at about 230 miles per second—fast enough to travel from New York City to Los Angeles in eleven seconds. The sun is actually traveling through the Local Interstellar Cloud, which is in the Local Bubble, which is in the Orion Arm, which is in the Milky Way, which is in the Local Group, which is in the Virgo Supercluster, which is only one of millions of superclusters in the observable universe.

3 # Bullsh*t!

The sun actually does not have enough mass to explode as a supernova. We do have a reason to worry, however, and less time to prepare. The sun will heat up and expand, and in about 5 billion years, it will officially become a red giant. Although our planet will not be blown up, it will likely be swallowed up by this enormous version of the sun. If Earth is spared that fate, it will only have to deal with minor inconveniences: The oceans will boil away and the atmosphere will escape.

"FACTS":
Gold!

1 In some cultures, people eat powdered gold, sprinkling it on fruit and other food items. The practice is harmless.

2 Gold is extremely *ductile*, which means it can be hammered into a very thin layer without breaking. Gold is so ductile that it would take less than 4 pounds of gold to stretch a wire from Los Angeles to New York City.

3 Ambergris, better known as "apple glass," is an expensive golden-hued decorative material made by mixing gold with molten glass.

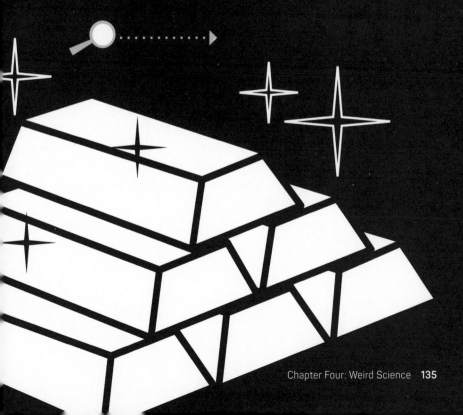

1 **Fact.** However, gold has no nutritional value, and it can't be digested. It just, you know, passes on through.

2 **Fact.** According to the American Museum of Natural History, 1 ounce of gold could be spun into gold wire 50 miles long and 5 microns thick. It would only take 49 ounces of gold—just slightly over 3 pounds—to stretch a wire from New York City to Los Angeles, which are roughly 2,450 miles apart. Of course, 5 microns thick means a wire so thin you wouldn't be able to see it.

3 # Bullsh*t!

As Victorian glassblowers knew, when you mix gold (or more accurately, gold chloride) with molten glass, the result is cranberry glass, which is an expensive glass that is visually striking thanks to its deep, rich, red hue. Ambergris, on the other hand, is a smelly, waxy substance produced in the digestive system of sperm whales and is regurgitated.

"FACTS":
Pi!

1 As of 2023, the Guinness World Record for pi memorization is held by an Indian man who successfully recited pi to 70,000 places. It took him nearly ten hours to recite. A Ukrainian man was recognized in 2006 by the *Book of Records of Ukraine* for having memorized pi to 1 million places.

2 In 2010, a Japanese man set a world record by calculating the value of pi to a billion decimal places. He managed this feat on his own personal laptop, which took a week to finish the job.

3 Givenchy markets a cologne named Pi, calling it "the thinking man's fragrance."

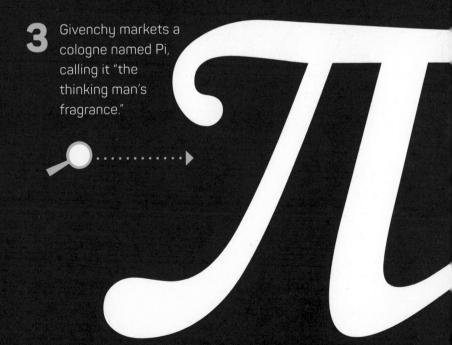

1 **Fact.** Rajveer Meena recited 70,000 digits in 2015 while blindfolded. Andriy Slyusarchuk, a Ukrainian neurosurgeon, was not content at 1 million. In 2009, he claimed to have pi memorized to 30 million places. Although recitation is not possible, he reportedly was able to recite any random selection of the digits asked of him. He was rewarded with a visit from (the now former) Ukrainian president Viktor Yushchenko.

2 # Bullsh*t!

In 2010, Japanese system engineer Shigeru Kondo and American computer science student Alexander Yee set a world record by calculating pi to 5 trillion decimal places. Kondo built a powerful computer specifically for the task that cost $18,000 in parts, including twenty external hard drives. The process took more than ninety days. Google Cloud has since set the new world record in 2022, calculating pi to over 100 trillion digits.

3 **Fact.** Givenchy's Pi is a "modern masculine blend of tangerine, neroli, rosemary, and tarragon." Smells like smarts!

"FACTS":
Pee!

1 From the seventeenth to the nineteenth centuries, stale human urine was a common household product. The aged pee, called lant, had multiple uses, including cleaning floors and rinsing hair. It was also used as an additive to ale, and as an ingredient in pastries.

2 Pee has less bacteria and fewer microorganisms than the water coming out of your kitchen faucet.

3 Human urine is high in acetic acid, which has the peculiar quality of neutralizing the sting of a jellyfish. A jellyfish encounter with the skin leaves behind tiny stingers, which can keep firing long after the jellyfish is gone. Acetic acid causes the stingers to shut down. For this reason, urinating on a jellyfish sting is the best thing one can do for pain relief.

1 **Fact.** Lant has a high ammonia content, making it great for cleaning. It was often used as a hair rinse, and you can still find urea listed on many shampoo bottles (though today, the urea is synthetic). Apparently, some hardcore pub crawlers of the time loved the flavor of pee in their brew—ale could be single- or double-lanted, according to taste. Plus, lant was used in pastry recipes to help the glaze stick.

2 **Fact.** Urine is sterile when it comes out of your kidneys. It only becomes contaminated after contact with bacteria on your skin—or if you have an infection.

3 # Bullsh*t!

It's an old wives' tale. Some people have reported relief from peeing on a jellyfish sting and many others have not. According to scientists, urinating on a sting can actually make the pain worse. Urine does not contain acetic acid—that's the primary ingredient of vinegar, which is also touted as a remedy for jellyfish stings. Jellyfish stings *do* leave behind tiny stingers, called nematocysts, which can continue to inject venom after the jellyfish is gone. Acetic acid (from vinegar) can neutralize the nematocysts in some jellyfish stings but can make things worse in others. Any change in the balance of solutes (i.e., saltiness) can cause nematocysts to sting. For this reason, rinsing the sting with fresh water is not recommended. Urine is largely fresh water, which will result in a fresh stinging sensation.

"FACTS":
P!

1 P is the symbol for the chemical element phosphorus, which has the atomic number 15. Phosphorus can be distilled from urine.

2 p is the symbol for momentum in physics. Momentum is the product of the mass and velocity of an object. Therefore, $p = mv$.

3 P is the symbol for the Paratore constant, which is the magnitude of electric charge per mole of electrons. It is handy in the study of electrolysis.

1 **Fact.** Yes, P can be distilled from pee. Urine is high in phosphates. Phosphorus is a basic element and can be found on the periodic table of the elements, indicated by P and its atomic number, 15.

2 **Fact.** This is true in classical mechanics but gets much more complicated in relativistic mechanics, where you have to account for the Lorentz factor (Y). The formula in relativistic mechanics is $p = YmOv$.

3 # Bullsh*t!
The statement is true about the Faraday constant, which has the symbol F.

"FACTS":
Electrocution!

1 When the metal band Crowstone played a 2019 out-door concert in Harvey Park near Columbus, lightning struck the stage. Guitarists Gregory Rahm and Mike Leach were both electrocuted instantly and bassist Thomas Owens was knocked unconscious. Drummer Travis Kline escaped completely unscathed.

2 In the late nineteenth century, Thomas Edison presided over the electrocution deaths of numerous innocent stray dogs and cats, as well as a few cattle and horses. He concluded the gruesome demonstrations with the 1903 public electrocution of a Coney Island elephant named Topsy.

3 When murderer Pedro Medina was executed in 1997, the electric chair, Old Sparky, malfunctioned. Witnesses reported that foot-high flames shot from Medina's head.

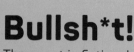

1 Bullsh*t!

The event is fictional. Gregory Rahm, Mike Leach, Thomas Owens, and Travis Kline are all members of the metal band Struck by Lightning. Crowstone and Harvey Park probably don't exist.

2 **Fact.** Edison was himself a proponent of DC current, as opposed to Nikola Tesla's AC current. He fried all the animals in question with AC current in hopes of convincing the public that it was too dangerous for household use. His efforts (and many animal lives) were in vain, and AC current became the standard shortly thereafter.

3 **Fact.** The case went on to prove a strong argument for the continued shift away from electric chairs and toward lethal injection for executions. But Florida attorney general Bob Butterworth found the sudden PR gratifying. "People who wish to commit murder, they better not do it in the state of Florida, because we may have a problem with our electric chair," he said.

"FACTS":
Dentistry!

1 Working in Pakistan in 2006, researchers from the University of Poitiers discovered dental tools and skulls that date back to 500 B.C.E., proving that sophisticated tooth extraction and dentistry was practiced more than 2,500 years ago.

2 The first dental school in the world was the Baltimore College of Dental Surgery, founded in 1840. The institution was the first to issue a Doctor of Dental Surgery degree (DDS) and is still in operation as part of the University of Maryland.

3 Contrary to popular assumption, our teeth are not made of bone. They are made up of four major components: enamel, dentin, cementum, and pulp. But no bone at all.

1 Bullsh*t!

The University of Poitiers team found out that dentistry is much older than 2,500 years. They discovered eleven molars from a Neolithic grave-yard in Pakistan with perfectly drilled holes, dating to 7000 B.C.E., indicating that sophisticated dentistry occurred more than 9,000 years ago. The prehistoric dentists used flint-tipped drills connected to rods and bowstrings to make holes that modern dentists have dubbed "amazing" in their quality. Anthropologists believe that the skill of the work might be due to the expert bead-working skills that prehistoric people of the area possessed. Smoothing of the teeth show that the patients continued to chew long after visiting the "dentist." Too bad that modern anesthesia wasn't invented until the nineteenth century.

2 **Fact.** BCDS was, in 1840, the first school in the world to offer a science-based education in dentistry. Dentistry was practiced long before that, which makes one wonder: Who taught those dentists? The second school was Philadelphia Dental College, founded in 1863. It's now a part of Temple University and was renamed the Kornberg School of Dentistry.

3 **Fact.** The visible part of our teeth is the enamel, which is the hardest substance in the human body. Underneath it is the dentin, a calcified tissue that is actually yellow in color. Cementum is a calcified substance that forms around the roots of our teeth. Finally, pulp is at the center of our teeth and is made up of living connective tissue and cells.

"FACTS":
Bacteria!

1 The bacteria *Escherichia coli*, commonly called *E. coli*, was discovered in 1933 by Antonie van Leeuwenhoek and named after the Dutch artist M.C. Escher. It is one of the most virulent strains of bacteria known. Being infected by even a tiny amount of *E. coli* will likely lead to major sickness including fever and diarrhea, and it carries life-threatening risks.

2 Anthrax, syphilis, cholera, leprosy, gonorrhea, Rocky Mountain spotted fever, and the bubonic plague are all caused by bacteria.

3 There are approximately 5 nonillion (5,000,000,000, 000,000,000,000,000,000,000) bacteria on the planet. There are more bacteria cells on or in your body than there are any other kind of cells making up your body.

Bullsh*t!

Escherichia coli was discovered by a pediatrician named Theodor Escherich in 1885 and was eventually named after him. Antonie van Leeuwenhoek was a seventeenth-century scientist who was the first to observe bacteria. Only certain strains of *E. coli* lead to food poisoning or sickness. In fact, *E. coli* exists harmlessly in the intestinal tract of most warm-blooded animals. Humans are typically colonized by *E. coli* within forty hours of birth, and the bacteria stick around until we die.

2 **Fact.** Those diseases and conditions, ranging from annoying to awful, are caused by the bacteria *Bacillus anthracis*, *Treponema pallidum*, *Vibrio cholerae*, *Mycobacterium leprae*, *Neisseria gonorrhoeae*, *Rickettsia rickettsii*, and *Yersinia pestis*, respectively.

3 **Fact.** The number of bacteria on the planet was estimated by the report "Prokaryotes: The Unseen Majority." The 5 nonillion bacteria represent a huge portion of the world's biomass. Scientists estimate that we have as many as ten times the number of bacteria as human cells in our body. In truth, we're just giant collections of bacteria walking around.

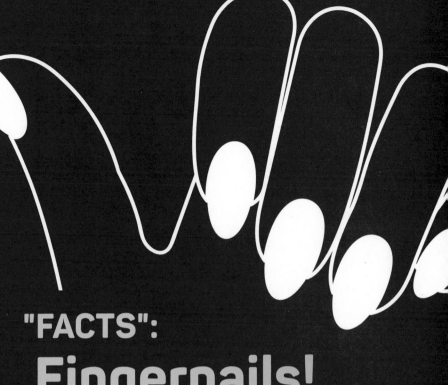

"FACTS":
Fingernails!

1 The record for the world's longest nails on a single hand belongs to Evgeny Kolyadintsev of Moscow, whose nails were over 6 feet long on his right hand.

2 Fingernails grow between three and four times faster than toenails. The nail on your index finger grows faster than the one on your pinkie.

3 Fingernails and hair are made of the same substance, keratin.

1 Bullsh*t!

The record for the world's longest nails on a single hand belongs to Shridhar Chillal of India, whose nails were over 20 feet long on his left hand (his hand became disfigured from carrying around the weight, and he got out the nail trimmers in 2000). The record for the world's longest fingernails on both hands belongs to Diana Armstrong from Minnesota, whose nails were over 42 feet long in total. She refuses to cut them as a tribute to her deceased daughter, Latisha, who was her personal nail artist.

2 **Fact.** The speed of nail growth directly corresponds to the length of the actual finger or toe. The longer the bone, the faster the nail grows.

3 **Fact.** Fingernails and hair are both made up of a protein called keratin. It's also the main ingredient in the outer layer of your skin. Keratin comes in both soft and hard varieties, which is why your hair can be so soft and bouncy and your nails can be as tough as, well, nails. Certain fungi eat keratin, which is why it can be hard to get rid of athlete's foot.

"FACTS":
Lasers!

1 The term "laser" began as an acronym. LASER stood for "light amplification by stimulated emission of radiation." Less well known, but equally important, is the maser, which also comes from an acronym ("microwave amplification by stimulated emission of radiation"). The maser emits coherent microwave radiation, while the laser emits coherent visible or infrared light radiation.

2 Researchers at Harvard have managed to control the actions of worms without wires or electrodes, using nothing but laser light. The system they designed is known as the "CoLBeRT" ("Controlling Locomotion and Behavior in Real-Time") after TV personality Stephen Colbert.

3 Although laser weapons are common in science fiction, at our current level of technological advancement, any kind of actual laser weapon is impossible. Lasers can be used to enhance weapons (laser scope) or even to trigger them, but laser light itself cannot hurt or kill.

1 **Fact.** The maser was actually invented first. When the laser was invented, the term "optical maser" was suggested, but "laser" was adopted instead.

2 **Fact.** The researchers at Harvard's Center for Brain Science genetically modified the neurons of nematode worms, favoring worms with an inherent gene that produces light-sensitive ion channel proteins. The worms are "programmed" to respond to different wavelengths of light with different actions (such as turning left, stopping, etc.).

3 # Bullsh*t!

Even a laser pointer can hurt (particularly if it hits your retina). The Air Force initiated the YAL-1 Airborne Laser system in 1996. The YAL-1 is a giant laser mounted on a Boeing 747, designed to destroy airborne tactical ballistic missiles. In January 2010, the system successfully destroyed two test missiles. The ZEUS laser was the first laser weapon deployed by the military and was used with great success in the Iraq War, although primarily to heat up and detonate land mines. The Mobile Tactical High-Energy Laser, or MTHEL, was developed by the US military and Israel; it was designed to shoot down missiles and aircrafts. Handheld laser guns are not around yet because of the extraordinary power they would need to operate. Laser beams themselves can heat and cut (such as in LASIK eye surgery). In 1995, the United Nations issued the Protocol on Blinding Laser Weapons, which bans the use of lasers to blind enemies.

"FACTS":
Hiccups!

1 Forget holding your breath or drinking a glass of water upside down. Medical studies have unveiled an unlikely but effective treatment for uncontrollable hiccups: digital rectal massage.

2 Iowa farmer Charles Osborne had the hiccups during waking hours for sixty-eight years. Until his death in 1991, it's estimated he hiccupped 500 million times.

3 The word "hiccup" comes from the Latin *hic*, which means "breath."

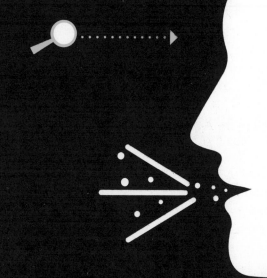

1 **Fact.** Yes, "digital" as in fingers, and "rectal" as in butt. There are a handful of cases in which a "rectal massage" has shown to cure hiccups. It seems this discovery was a happy accident. A sixty-year-old man was admitted to the hospital with acute pancreatitis and was immediately fitted with a nasogastric tube. Hiccups commenced and continued for two days. Multiple treatments were attempted (including a spoonful of sugar) to no avail. Finally, during a routine rectal examination, the hiccups abruptly stopped. A few hours later, they began again. The rectal exam was repeated, and the hiccups again stopped. A report from the Bnai Zion Medical Center in Haifa, Israel, called "Termination of Intractable Hiccups with Digital Rectal Massage," outlines the details of this new and exciting remedy.

2 **Fact.** Despite traveling to doctors all over the country to look for a solution, Osborne never encountered a permanent solution to his hiccups, which began in his late twenties. He hiccupped about twenty times a minute, on average, for nearly seven decades. The hiccups subsided each night as he slept, only to return in the morning.

3 # Bullsh*t!

The word "hiccup," alternately spelled "hiccough," is actually an onomatopoeia from the seventeenth century. (An onomatopoeia is a word that, accidentally or on purpose, sounds like its meaning.) Invented to describe the sound of a hiccup, the word has no relation to previous words or languages. *Hic* is the Latin word for "here."

"FACTS":
Viagra!

1 Viagra's not just for bedroom performance: Professional athletes use the drug to enhance their athletic ability, and the little blue pills have been investigated as to whether they should be considered performance-enhancing and therefore be banned.

2 Sildenafil was first developed at Pfizer as a treatment for hypertension and angina. During its clinical trials, researchers noticed that the drug was ineffective for treating those conditions, but that it was producing penile erections. Subsequently, they decided to market it for erectile dysfunction.

3 Sildenafil is a crystalline tropane alkaloid which inhibits phyllosilicate hydroxyl ($Al_2Si_2O_5(OH)_4$), a protein which regulates blood flow to the penis. Besides Viagra, sildenafil has been marketed under the brand names Levitra, Vivanza, and Cialis.

1 **Fact.** According to the *New York Daily News*, anonymous sources report that baseball players Roger Clemens and Barry Bonds used the drug to enhance on-field performance, and Italian cyclist Andrea Moletta was accused of "doping" with Viagra. Major League Baseball and the Giro d'Italia do not specifically ban Viagra, but the World Anti-Doping Agency investigated the idea that the drug would enhance athletic ability. Some Viagra experts assert that the drug would have very little benefit to athletes and that any benefit would be a case of the placebo effect.

2 **Fact.** The drug was patented in 1996 and approved by the FDA as a treatment for erectile dysfunction in 1998. It was the first-ever oral treatment for ED. Although not particularly effective as a treatment for regular hypertension and angina, the drug has been approved as a treatment for pulmonary hypertension and is marketed for that purpose under the name Revatio.

3 # Bullsh*t!

Viagra is not a crystalline tropane alkaloid, but a much more dangerous drug—cocaine—is. It's not a phyllosilicate, which is a mineral, and it is not $Al_2Si_2O_5(OH)_4$—that's the chemical representation of dickite. Sildenafil is a selective inhibitor of cyclic guanosine monophosphate (cGMP)-specific phosphodiesterase type 5 (PDE5), an enzyme that regulates blood flow to the penis. Sildenafil is marketed as Viagra, but Levitra and Vivanza are brand names for vardenafil, and Cialis is a brand name for tadalafil.

"FACTS":
The Milky Way!

1 The official name is the Milky Way Galaxy, which is actually redundant in a way: The word "galaxy" comes from the post-classical Latin *galaxias*, which means "milky way." The Greek root *gala* means "milk."

2 The Milky Way is the galaxy we live in, and at its center is a supermassive black hole named Sagittarius A*. The entire galaxy is 100,000 light-years in diameter, and our sun is just one of the estimated 200–400 billion stars in it.

3 English is the only language in which we refer to the galaxy as the "Milky Way." In other languages it is known as the "Diamond Finger," the "Thousand Layers of Paper," the "Iron Shirt," the "Deity's Palm," and the "Nephrite Belt."

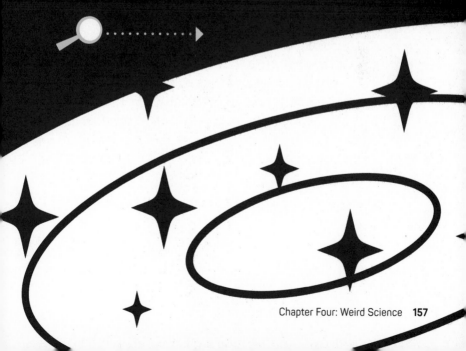

1 **Fact.** The ancients dubbed our galaxy the Milky Way because of the visible milky patches of night sky, which were actually millions of stars. A Greek version of the word "milk" is *galaktos*.

2 **Fact.** Sagittarius A* (pronounced "A-Star") has the asterisk because there is technically no way to *prove* that the black hole is there, although most space experts believe it is. Sagittarius A* is only about 26,000 light-years from the earth. One hundred thousand light-years is incredibly wide. It's 587,862,537,318,360,800 miles! It's shaped like a disk too. Depending on what you're measuring, it's only between 2,000 and 12,000 light-years across. If you think an estimation of between 200 and 400 billion stars is pretty broad, you're right. We still have plenty to learn about our home galaxy.

3 # Bullsh*t!

All of those are moves or skills in Shaolin kung fu. Many other languages call our galaxy the Milky Way, but there are a lot of creative names as well that derive from ancient legends: In Cherokee, it is *Gi`li`-utsûñ'stänûñ'yi*, or "Where the Dog Ran." In Hungarian, it is *Hadak Útja*, or the "Way of the Warriors."

"FACTS":
Mind Control!

1 In 1999, a team led by Yang Dan at the University of California, Berkeley, managed to control the mind of a cat with a complex series of electrodes directly connected to the cat's brain. The team was able to make Bella sit, stand, walk, and turn both left and right with commands entered into a keyboard.

2 A team at the Freie Universität Berlin has produced a car that you can drive with your mind. The program is called BrainDriver.

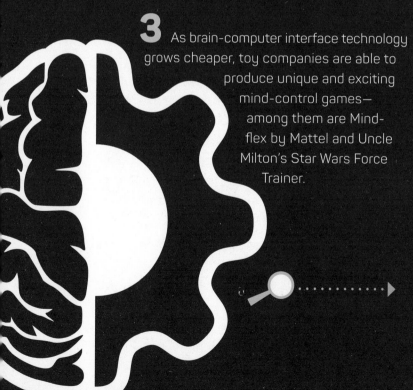

3 As brain-computer interface technology grows cheaper, toy companies are able to produce unique and exciting mind-control games— among them are Mind-flex by Mattel and Uncle Milton's Star Wars Force Trainer.

1 Bullsh*t!

That would be cruel. Yang Dan's team at UCB did do something awesome with cats, however: They decoded "messages" from firing neurons in cats' brains and were able to produce images and movies of what the cats see. How cool!

2 **Fact.** The team, led by Raúl Rojas, tricked out a Volkswagen Passat with some serious technological bling. The primary equipment is the driver's headset, which is wirelessly connected to a computer interface. The headset measures electromagnetic signals from the brain, which, after calibration, mean different things to the software. Hence, the driver can think "slow down" or "turn left" and watch the car comply. The Passat is also outfitted with video cameras, radars, and laser sensors that help the car "know" its surroundings and help the driver with adjustments, such as the severity of a turn, for example. Unfortunately, the mind-controlled car is not street ready: There is a short delay between the thought and the car's execution of that thought (not something you want on the highway), and it's still not possible to apply a lot of detail to your instructions to the car.

3 **Fact.** Both toys used electroencephalography (EEG) technology to read your brain waves. With an EEG headset, you can control the speed of a fan, which blows a Styrofoam ball into the air, giving the illusion of telekinesis. The Star Wars Force Trainer comes with the added delight of hearing Yoda's voice praise your performance.

"FACTS":
Flamethrowers!

1 Concerned about the potential for disastrous floods as a result of heavy snowfall, the mayor of Boston, James Curley, sent a letter to the president of the Massachusetts Institute of Technology, asking him to assign a group of engineers to the task of melting snow drifts. The mayor's suggestion? Flamethrowers.

2 Detroit inventor Charl Fourie unveiled a hood-mounted flamethrower for cars (maintaining that it was intended for self-defense only) and received thousands of orders. Unfortunately, he was prevented from fulfilling them due to a federal law that made personal possession of flamethrowers illegal.

3 The modern flamethrower was invented in the early twentieth century, but massive tubed flamethrowers were used as early as 424 B.C.E., and the Byzantine navy had sophisticated brass-tubed flamethrowers mounted on their ships by C.E. 672.

1 **Fact.** In 1948, the new year brought massive snowfall with it, and Mayor Curley was apparently desperate. Nothing can go wrong by unleashing flamethrowers on the Boston streets, right? His idea was perhaps not that far-fetched. Today you can buy the BareBlaster Propane Ice Torch and scorch the h*ll out of your driveway.

2 # Bullsh*t!

Fourie did invent a vehicle flamethrower, called the Blaster, in 1998 in his native South Africa. The Blaster was not hood-mounted but spewed flame from underneath the side doors (for the purpose of deterring carjackers). His first customer was a police superintendent, and he received a lot of media attention, but in the end, he only sold a few hundred units before moving on to his next invention: a pocket-sized personal flamethrower. By the way, in the US, there is no federal law against private individuals owning flamethrowers.

3 **Fact.** Ancient Greek historian Thucydides wrote about a massive siege engine built by the Boeotians, in which a bellows propelled air up a hollowed-out beam of wood and into a cauldron filled with flammable resin; the Boeotians would then direct the flames, spouting fire on enemy fortifications. This was used to devastating effect against the Athenians in the Battle of Delium in 424 B.C.E. The Byzantine naval flamethrowers were dominant and effective, winning for them multiple sea battles during the Arab-Byzantine wars. The modern flamethrower was invented by German scientist Richard Fiedler in 1901.

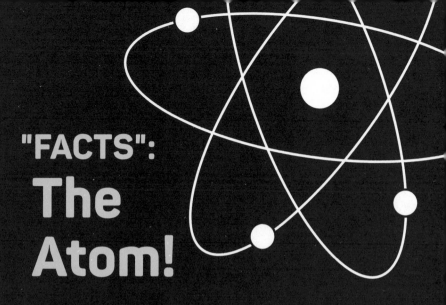

"FACTS":
The Atom!

1 The atom is made up of subatomic particles called electrons, protons, and neutrons. Electrons are the lightweights of the bunch: It takes more than 1,800 of them to equal the mass of one proton.

2 An atom is so small that it would take roughly a quadrillion (1,000,000,000,000,000) hydrogen atoms to tip the scales at 1 pound. A human hair is about 10 million carbon atoms thick. An estimated 2×10^{30} atoms make up the earth.

3 Nuclear fission is a nuclear reaction during which the nucleus of an atom splits apart. Fission can cause an exponentially growing nuclear chain reaction, something the world has experienced firsthand in the form of the atomic bomb.

1 **Fact.** Protons and neutrons have about the same mass, and they significantly outweigh electrons. If an electron had the mass of a small jelly bean, a proton would weigh the same as a 2-liter bottle of Diet Coke!

2

Bullsh*t!

Too heavy, too narrow, and too few. It would take nearly 300 septillion (300,000,000,000,000,000, 000,000,000) hydrogen atoms to weigh a pound. A human hair is only about 1 million carbon atoms thick. Written out, 2×10^{30} would be a 2 with 30 zeroes after it (2,000,000,000,000,000,000,000, 000,000,000), or 2 nonillion. In truth, Jefferson Labs estimates that the earth has 1.33×10^{50} atoms, or 133 quindecillion, which looks like this: 133,000,000,000,000,000,000,000,000,000,000, 000,000,000,000,000,000,000.

3 **Fact.** When the nucleus of an atom is split (an act known as "fission"), the fragments rapidly travel away from one another. In an atomic bomb, neutrons freed by the split collide with other nuclei, causing them to split in a successive exponential chain reaction. The motion of all the fragments traveling so quickly apart from one another is converted to X-ray heat, which is what makes the bomb so destructive.

"FACTS":
Magnets!

1 Magnets were first discovered in ancient Greece. Naturally occurring magnetized minerals called lodestones were used to make the first magnetic compasses; lodestones were also prized for their "magical" properties.

2 While the very first credit cards were magnetic, these days the "magnetic strip" on the back of your credit card is not actually magnetic at all. The strip is made of injection-molded plastic, which stores information in a series of tiny bumps and valleys.

3 In a groundbreaking 2010 study, neuro-scientists at the Massachusetts Institute of Technology discovered that magnets can alter your sense of morality. When participants' brains were subjected to strong magnetic fields, they were more likely to judge a morally dubious scenario as acceptable, and vice versa.

1 **Fact.** Lodestones are made of magnetite, which is partly iron. These lodestones were found in Magnesia, so they were called *magnetis lithos*, for "Magnesian stone." Over the years, the word simplified to "magnet" and entered our language that way.

2 Bullsh*t!

Injection-molded plastic with information stored in miniscule bumps and valleys is the mechanism at work with audio CDs. The first credit cards were not magnetic at all—they were like business cards with a person's account information written on it, allowing that person to use credit at a specific store. Today, the strip on the back of your credit card is, in fact, made up of thousands of tiny magnets encased in plastic.

3 **Fact.** The scientists used the magnetic fields to target the part of the brain that has been linked to moral judgment. When volunteers were subjected to the magnetic fields, they had a harder time separating intentions and outcomes in hypothetical scenarios. For example, when told that a woman tried to poison her friend, but the friend wasn't harmed, magnetized brains were more likely to judge the situation as morally acceptable.

"FACTS":
Blood!

1 One of the primary functions of our blood is to carry oxygen from the lungs to other parts of the body. When our blood is carrying oxygen, it is bright red. When it is not, our blood is a much darker red, with slight traces of blue. In general, our blood is never totally blue, and neither are our veins—the appearance is an optical illusion.

2 A biotech company formally called Arteriocyte had come up with a way to produce synthetic blood by "farming" it from umbilical cords. The hope was that the process could eliminate the need for donating blood in the near future.

3 There are about 8 gallons of blood in the human body. It would take 68 million mosquito bites to completely drain the average human of blood.

1 **Fact.** Our blood is red because of hemoglobin, an iron-rich protein in our red blood cells. The presence of oxygen makes those cells an even brighter red. It's a myth that deoxygenated blood is true blue—it is maroon, albeit sometimes with a bluish tinge. Some veins appear blue because of the complex way our skin absorbs and reflects light, but amazingly, they are not actually blue. If you weren't looking at them through your skin, you'd see them for what they are. Blood, by the way, is 55 percent plasma, which on its own is yellow.

2 **Fact.** Arteriocyte's (now called Isto Biologics) technology took hematopoietic cells from umbilical cords and put them in a bone marrow–like environment, with all the nutrients needed to become blood cells. In three days, 20 units of transfusion-ready blood was produced by 1 unit of umbilical cord blood. The discovery was financed by the Department of Defense. Mass-produced synthetic blood could be much more easily delivered to battlefields than donated blood, which needs to travel farther and can expire before it arrives. Blood loss is the cause of 40 percent of military casualties in the first twenty-four hours after injury. This research of creating synthetic blood still continues, with rapidly increasing results every year.

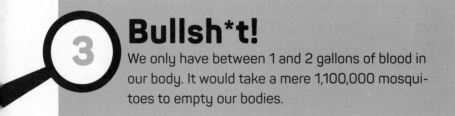

3 # Bullsh*t!
We only have between 1 and 2 gallons of blood in our body. It would take a mere 1,100,000 mosquitoes to empty our bodies.

"FACTS":
Uranus!

1 In our solar system, Uranus is the third-largest planet in terms of volume and the fourth-largest in terms of mass. Uranus is the coldest of the planets; if you lived near one of the poles on Uranus, you would have forty-two years of sunlight followed by forty-two years of darkness.

2 Uranus has thirteen known moons; the largest are named after characters from Homer's *Odyssey*, and/or Greek mythology: Odysseus, Penelope, Poseidon, Athena, and Calypso. All five major moons are made of solid rock.

3 Uranus has been visited only once, by a spacecraft called *Voyager 2*. It visited the Uranian system in 1986; recently, NASA has questioned the idea of visiting the icy planet. *Voyager 2* was launched in 1977 and still communicates with Earth.

1 **Fact.** Jupiter and Saturn take up much more space than Uranus. Neptune takes up less space but has more mass because it is denser. Uranus has the peculiar property of rotating on an axis that is drastically different from the other planets in our system. Because of this, one pole spends forty-two years in the sun (half of the time it takes the planet to orbit the sun) and forty-two years in darkness.

2 # Bullsh*t!

Uranus has twenty-seven known moons (and counting). The five major ones are named after characters from Shakespeare and Alexander Pope: Titania, Oberon, Ariel, Umbriel, and Miranda. All five moons are made of rock and ice (Miranda is predominantly ice). The rest of Uranus's moons take their names from Pope and Shakespeare as well, including Ophelia, Juliet, Desdemona, Portia, and Prospero. Odysseus, besides being the hero of the *Odyssey*, is a crater on Saturn's moon Tethys, and Penelope is as well. Poseidon is an asteroid and was once the name of a moon of Jupiter. Athene (not Athena) is an asteroid, and Calypso is a moon of Saturn.

3 **Fact.** In its first twelve years of operation, *Voyager 2* visited Jupiter, Saturn, Uranus, and Neptune, taking the first and most detailed pictures of each. There is still active communication between NASA and *Voyager 2* even though it is more than 8 billion miles away. Scientists have been attempting to secure funding for a trip to the blue planet.

CHAPTER FIVE

Sports and Other Activities

"FACTS":
The Football!

1 The football is commonly referred to as a *pigskin* because similar games were played in medieval Europe, using an inflated pig's bladder as the ball. Pig bladders were used for the inside of rugby balls as late as the nineteenth century. Modern American footballs were never made out of the actual *skin* of a pig.

2 Although footballs are iconic to America, official NFL game balls are actually made in China. The process is automated; making modern-day footballs by hand would be too difficult and dangerous for human workers. American-made footballs have not appeared in a Super Bowl since 1941!

3 In the NFL, no fewer than thirty-six footballs must be provided for each outdoor game. They are inspected and pressure tested by referees two hours before the game. A minimum of twelve footballs exclusively for kicking must also be provided, shipped in a special tamper-proof box from the manufacturer that can only be opened by a referee.

1 **Fact.** The medieval sport was often referred to as "foot ball" and also called "mob ball," which was appropriate because there were few rules. A rubber bladder for the inside of rugby balls and footballs was developed in the mid-1800s because people were getting infected by diseased pig's bladders when they inflated them *by mouth*. Modern footballs are typically made of cow leather or rubber.

2 # Bullsh*t!

In fact, NFL game balls are still made by hand in a small Wilson factory in Ada, Ohio. Every game ball since 1941 has been made there. The factory produces around 4,000 footballs per day, 365 days a year.

3 **Fact.** Thirty-six footballs are required for outdoor games, and twenty-four for indoor. They are each tested with a pressure gauge two hours before the game. When it comes to the twelve kicking footballs, the NFL goes so far as to stipulate that each ball must be marked with a K, and the case containing them can only be opened in the officials' locker room. This is to combat the fact that, in the past, kickers were roughing up their game balls, making them softer, slightly larger, and easier to kick.

"FACTS":
Jousting!

1 In a joust, competitors race their horses in a straight line toward each other, using their lances to unseat one another. A fence between them, called a tilt, keeps them from running into each other. The origin of the phrase "tilting at windmills"—meaning to joust or fight for an imaginary or ridiculous reason—originates from the word "tilt."

2 In 2017, a jousting accident at the Texas Renaissance Festival left competitor Trevor MacDermid with a fractured skull, brain swelling, and an *inability to speak English*. Even after four surgeries and years of therapy, the Brit still can't understand or speak his first language but is able to communicate by *speaking French*.

3 Bicycle jousting has emerged as a popular underground sport, with regular competitions in New York City and other major cities. Competitors compete on asphalt or pavement with spears made of metal or PVC pipe, and often on customized, extra-tall bikes. Injuries are common.

1 **Fact.** True, all true. In Cervantes's famous novel, *Don Quixote*, the titular hero imagines the arms of a windmill to be those of a giant, and he decides to attack the monstrous creature. His somewhat saner sidekick, Sancho, tries to dissuade him.

2 # Bullsh*t!
Can you imagine if that actually happened?

3 **Fact.** Brooklyn's Black Label Bike Club is considered to be the originators of the "sport," staging jousting competitions at its annual Bike Kill events. Some compete on mutant "tall bikes" that put them more than 8 feet in the air. That's a long way to fall. Other fun-for-the-whole-family competitions at underground events include: bicycle-tossing; chugging a six-pack of beer while riding; and the Whiplash, during which a rope is tied around the waist of two bicyclists, who then pedal away from each other as fast as they can. You can imagine the result.

"FACTS": The NBA!

1 Perhaps the most significant year for the NBA was 1979. During that year, the NBA adopted the three-pointer, and rookies Larry Bird and Magic Johnson joined the organization. These three factors reversed the major decline in popularity that the sport and the league were suffering.

2 At the time this book went to press, the record for most points ever scored by a single player in an NBA game is 100, held by legendary player Wilt Chamberlain; the record for most total points ever scored in an NBA game is 370, in a game between the Nuggets and the Pistons.

3 The National Basketball Association was created in 1936, and by the 1953–1954 basketball season, it had a whopping twenty-six franchises based in cities large and small. Of the twenty-six from that year, only one is still operational today: the New York Knickerbockers.

1 **Fact.** The three-point field goal was adopted from the American Basketball Association, a former rival of the NBA. Earvin "Magic" Johnson was selected first overall in the 1979 draft by the Lakers. Larry Bird was actually drafted in 1978 (sixth overall) by the Boston Celtics but waited a year before he signed in order to play his last year of college at Indiana State. Bird and Johnson's rivalry, and the added excitement from the three-point game, shook the NBA out of the slump it had been in during most of the '70s, when it was plagued by low attendance and poor ratings.

2 **Fact.** Wilt Chamberlain of the Philadelphia Warriors scored 100 points in his team's 169–147 win against the Knicks on March 2, 1962. That 316-point game was also an NBA record until the Detroit Pistons' 186–184 win over the Denver Nuggets on December 13, 1983. The game went into triple overtime.

3 # Bullsh*t!

In the 1953–1954 NBA season, there were only eight franchises, all of which are operational today: the Celtics, Knicks, Hawks, Lakers, Nationals/76ers, Pistons, Royals/Kings, and Warriors. The Basketball Association of America was founded in 1946, and it merged with the smaller National Basketball League in 1949 to create the NBA. The new league began with seventeen franchises from cities large and small, and then went through a consolidation process until it had only eight, the smallest number there would ever be.

"FACTS":
Volleyball!

1 Since 1971, the White Thorn Lodge in western Pennsylvania has hosted a wildly popular volleyball tournament annually. Over ninety teams typically participate, including high-quality players from around the world, such as Division 1 players, national team members, and European pros. One thing sets the tournament apart from all the others, however: The White Thorn Lodge is nudist, and all the participants play naked.

2 Volleyball was not included in the Olympics until the 1936 Berlin Games. The US team easily took the gold, and the United States vs. Germany game was famously attended by Adolf Hitler.

3 Volleyball was invented in 1895 by a YMCA physical education instructor in Holyoke, Massachusetts. The original name for the sport was "mintonette."

1 **Fact.** It's called the Superbowl of Naked Volleyball, and it's held at White Thorn every year during the first weekend after Labor Day. More than 1,500 players and naked volleyball fans show up.

2 # Bullsh*t!

Volleyball's official debut was in the 1964 Olympics in Tokyo. The gold went to the USSR. Volleyball was part of a demonstration of American sports in the 1924 Summer Olympics in Paris, but there were no formal competitions. Hitler attended the 1936 Berlin Games, but there was no volleyball played.

3 **Fact.** William G. Morgan invented the game for his classes of businessmen who were looking for an indoor sport less rough than basketball but still requiring rigorous activity. (Basketball had been invented only four years before at another YMCA in Springfield, only 10 miles away!) It isn't confirmed why Morgan called it "mintonette." An observer at an 1896 game noted the amount of volleying going on, and the sport was renamed "volley ball," which has since been fused into the one word we use today.

"FACTS":
Luge!

1 Luge was invented in the 1870s by a Swiss entrepreneur named Caspar Badrutt, who was looking for activities to entice travelers to his hotel in the winter.

2 Luge has been an Olympic sport since 1964. Germany has almost dominated the event since the beginning, winning eighty-one medals. On seven occasions, Germany swept an Olympic luge event, supplying all three medalists on the podium. No other country has even done that once. The United States has only won six medals in luge competition: three silvers and three bronzes.

3 Luge events in the 2010 Winter Olympics were held at the Whistler Sliding Centre in British Columbia. Competitors complained that the forty-year-old track was too slow and recorded some of the worst times in the history of luge competition.

1 **Fact.** Badrutt's hotel in St. Moritz, Switzerland, became one of the first winter resorts. Before Badrutt's influence, it was not a normal practice to spend the winter someplace cold. The story goes that guests began using delivery sleds for their own recreational use (their items would be dragged through the snow on sleds), which resulted in numerous collisions and accidents with people on the mountain. Badrutt organized rules and events around the idea of sledding, and the luge was born. Badrutt's resort also paved the way for modern-day recreational skiing.

2 **Fact.** It's hard to say what makes Germans so incredible at sliding around on their backs. Maybe it's something in the water. Austria's in second place, with twenty-two medals. Several countries participate that have never medaled, including France, Japan, and Switzerland.

3 # Bullsh*t!

The track was relatively new, with the first run taking place in 2007, and produced the fastest luge speeds ever recorded. The highest speed belonged to Manuel Pfister of Austria, who clocked in at 154 kilometers per hour (about 96 miles per hour). The track was so fast that it led to a fatality: Georgian luger Nodar Kumaritashvili flew off the track during a training run and collided with a steel pole. Despite its dangerous profile, deaths during luge are relatively rare. Kumaritashvili's death was the first since 1975.

"FACTS":
Archery!

1 In archery, a certain kind of target is called a "butt," which is where the expression "butt of the joke" comes from.

2 When shooting at a target with a traditional bow, you do not want to aim directly at the bull's-eye. In order to strike the center, you need to aim the arrow a little to one side.

3 The technical term for a fan of archery is "arctophile."

1 **Fact.** Reassure yourself with the knowledge that, when you're the butt of a joke, you're merely a target.

2 **Fact.** This phenomenon is known as the "archer's paradox." A right-handed archer should aim to the left of the target, and vice versa. Even though an arrow feels rigid, it flexes quite a bit when it is released. The bowstring moves just a little bit sideways when the archer's fingers let go, which causes the arrow to flex accordingly. This is good, since it helps the arrow stay clear of the bow itself when it takes off. After that first flex, the arrow will flex the other way, turning it back on course. The arrow in flight continuously oscillates, flexing slightly less each time, until it finds its mark.

3 # Bullsh*t!

An arctophile is someone who loves teddy bears. An archery buff is a toxophilite. The term was coined in the sixteenth century and comes from the Greek *toxon* for "bow" and *philos* for "loving."

"FACTS":
The Yo-Yo!

1 The yo-yo as a toy is extremely old. The National Archaeological Museum of Athens in Greece has a terra-cotta yo-yo that is dated to 500 B.C.E. There are drawings of yo-yos in ancient Egyptian temples.

2 The following are all legitimate yo-yo tricks: the Spirit Bomb, Skin the Gerbil, Kuru Milk, the Tidal Wave, the Kwyjibo, and the Iron Whip.

3 The yo-yo was used as a weapon for a long time. In the sixteenth century, hunters in the Philippines would sit in tree branches and strike their prey with a yo-yo. The word "yo-yo" actually comes from the Chinese *yuht yúh*, meaning "back."

1 **Fact.** The yo-yo goes way back! There's no telling who created the first yo-yo, but it is believed to have originated in China. Yo-yos were popular in Europe by the late eighteenth century, and the first yo-yos were largely produced in the US in 1866.

2 **Fact.** Though they may sound like superhero names or professional wrestling moves, all are official tricks according to the National Yo-Yo League.

3 # Bullsh*t!

It's a popular myth that the yo-yo was used as a weapon in the Philippines, but it's just not true. Filipino hunters in the sixteenth century would tie a rope to a rock, sit in a tree, and throw the rock at their prey. If they missed, they'd use the rope to haul the rock up again. The process calls to mind the yo-yo, sure, but a rock and a rope do not make a yo-yo. The word "yo-yo" is Filipino in origin. It is believed that the word comes from a Tagalog word meaning "return." (*Yuht yúh*, also called *Yue*, is a language in China and has no relation to "yo-yo.")

"FACTS":
The Frisbee!

1 The term "Frisbee" comes from a nineteenth-century baking company called the Frisbie Pie Company, founded by William Russell Frisbie. The word "Frisbee" is now a trademark of the Wham-O company; when it originally acquired the rights to a flying disc, it was called the Pluto Platter.

2 The first woman inducted into the World Frisbee Hall of Fame was Ashley Whippet, the California stuntwoman who is credited for initiating a major Frisbee craze after she performed incredible Frisbee catches and throws at a 1974 Dodgers game. Her acrobatic skills were featured in a critically acclaimed full-length documentary called *Throw It Away*.

3 Guts is a game in which two teams throw a Frisbee at each other, often with extreme velocity, in the hopes that the opposing team will fail to catch it. The sport is governed by the USGPA, or the United States Guts Players Association. Guts champions are crowned each year at the International Frisbee Tournament.

1 **Fact.** The Frisbie Pie Company was based out of Bridgeport, Connecticut. The company's pie tins (with the word "Frisbie" on them) were popular toys among local schoolboys. The idea to sell flying discs as toys came from Walter Frederick Morrison. His first design was called the Whirlo-Way, and his later design was called the Pluto Platter, the rights to which he sold to Wham-O. Wham-O rechristened it the Frisbee.

2

Bullsh*t!

Ashley Whippet *is* credited with helping to popularize Frisbee sports, and Ashley *did* perform amazing disc-catching stunts at Dodgers stadium, but Ashley was not a stuntwoman: He was a dog. On August 5, 1974, Ashley and his owner, Alex Stein, hopped the fence during a Dodgers-Reds game and immediately began performing stunts; Ashley caught the disc in a spectacular fashion. Stein was arrested, but their fame was established. Stein would go on to create the Frisbee Dog World Championship, which continues to this day. Ashley Whippet was the champion for the first three years. Ashley's skills were featured in an Academy Award–nominated short film called *Floating Free*.

3 **Fact.** The sport was developed in the 1960s and continues to gain popularity. The annual tournament routinely features teams from Japan. A noncompetitive version of the sport is known as "flutterguts."

"FACTS":
Lucha Libre!

1 Colorful masked characters engaging in mock battle
has been a tradition in Mexico since the days of the
Aztecs, and modern professional wrestling both in
the United States and Mexico spawned from the
long-venerated practice of lucha libre. Colorful *luchador* wrestling masks in the style
seen today made their first appearance in
the early nineteenth century.

2 The most famous lucha libre fighter of all
time was Rodolfo Guzmán Huerta, with
the stage name El Santo (The Saint).
True to the lucha libre mystique, Huerta
always appeared in public wearing his
silver mask, only revealing his face once
at the end of his career. Huerta appeared
in more than fifty lucha libre movies,
including the (translated) titles *Santo
vs. the Evil Brain*, *Santo vs. the Vampire
Women*, and *Santo in the Hotel of Death*.

3 Lucha libre wrestlers are generally divided into
two types: *rudos* and *técnicos*. The *rudos* are the
"bad guys" and *técnicos* are the "good guys." The three
lightest weight classes are *mosca*, *gallo*, and *pluma*.

1 Bullsh*t!

It is true that masks were a part of Aztec culture, but lucha libre masks did not evolve from Aztec masks. The sport is not ancient and is an off-shoot of professional wrestling, not the other way around. The first lucha libre masks were inspired by masked American professional wrestlers. The first major Mexican professional wrestling organization, Empresa Mexicana de Lucha Libre (EMLL), was founded in 1933, and the sport gained true popularity with the advent of TV in the 1950s. The mask phenomenon began when a masked American wrestler, Cyclone Mackey, fought in the EMLL. Fans loved the mystique, and the tradition was quickly adopted.

2 **Fact.** Huerta wrestled for nearly five decades and became an enormous celebrity and cultural icon in Mexico; he was the source of inspiration for an animated series, comic books, and many movies. He fought his last match just weeks before his sixty-fifth birthday. Huerta was buried wearing his silver mask.

3 **Fact.** As a general rule, the *rudos* (rude ones) will "break the rules" and employ a brawling style, while the *técnicos* (technicians) stick to the rules, play the part of the good guy, and display much more technical proficiency. *Mosca*, *gallo*, and *pluma* mean fly, rooster, and feather, respectively and directly correspond to the terms flyweight, bantamweight, and featherweight in combat sports.

"FACTS": The Baseball Glove!

1 While playing for the Chicago White Stockings, Hall of Fame pitcher Albert Goodwill Spalding became the first baseball star to wear a padded glove on his catching hand. Spalding had an ulterior motive: He manufactured gloves on the side and began to sell them like hotcakes. Today, his company, Spalding, is still a major sporting goods brand.

2 In the early days of American baseball, it was down-right unheard-of to wear a glove. When players tried out the first gloves (nonpadded, fingerless affairs), they were ridiculed. Even catchers played barehanded, and nearly all catches in a game were two-handed.

3 A Wake Forest University study on the minor leagues showed that catcher's gloves are extremely effective at protecting the hand. Players in this position have about the same rate of hand injuries as other baseball players, despite the fact that they catch more often.

1 **Fact.** Albert Goodwill Spalding was a pitcher for the Excelsior Club of Chicago, the Boston Red Stockings, and finally the Chicago White Stockings. While playing for the White Stockings in 1877, he opened a sporting goods store and began to manufacture baseballs and baseball gloves. He started to use a glove in games in order to promote them. Today, Spalding is headquartered in Springfield, Massachusetts, makes supplies for a variety of sports, and is probably best known for its basketballs.

2 **Fact.** A catcher named George Ellard immortalized the antiglove sentiment in his 1880 poem:

> We used no mattress on our hands,
> No cage upon our face;
> We stood right up and caught the ball
> With courage and with grace.

It was a stigma that was slow to disappear, but players, dealing with excruciating bruising, eventually prevailed over the mindset.

3 # Bullsh*t!

The study showed that seven of nine baseball catchers experience serious hypertrophy of the index finger (usually two ring-sizes bigger) and that the phenomenon only affected catchers. Forty-four percent of catchers had weakened catching hands due to trauma (compared to 17 percent of outfielders), and all of the catchers showed symptoms of nerve damage and abnormal blood flow.

"FACTS":
Ice Skating!

1 Ice skates were invented in 1831 by Finnish daredevil Renny Harlin. However, Finns have a long history of skating across the ice—2,000 years ago, they propelled themselves with sticks while standing on platter-shaped sleds called *valheita*.

2 Figure skating emerged as a popular sport in the second half of the nineteenth century, and the first international championship competition was held in 1896. At first, it was considered a men's sport only, and it was called "figure" skating because competitors had to draw perfect figures on the ice with their skates.

3 In 2009, a bear viciously attacked two men in Kyrgyzstan, killing one and severely injuring the other, before being shot dead by police. The bear was wearing ice skates at the time.

1 Bullsh*t!

Ice skates were invented by Finns, but it happened more than 5,000 years ago. In southern Finland, there are more lakes per unit of land area than anywhere else in the world, and the ancient Finns discovered that it was a lot more efficient to skate across a frozen lake than to walk around it. The first skates were simply animal bones tied to the feet. The Vikings became big adopters of the practice. Renny Harlin is the Finnish movie director who gave us *Cliffhanger* and *Die Hard 2*. *Valheita* is Finnish for "lies."

2 **Fact.** Figures weren't removed from competition until the '90s.

3 **Fact.** The bear was one of many famous Russian circus bears that have been trained to ice skate and even play hockey. The bear might have decided he was sick of skating, however, when he attacked and killed the circus director. One of the bear's trainers was critically injured when he heroically tried to intervene.

"FACTS":
Tug-of-War!

1 The first Black athlete to ever compete in the modern Olympics was Haitian-born Constantin Henriquez de Zubiera, who competed for France in the 1900 Games. De Zubiera helped France earn a silver medal in a unique sport: tug-of-war.

2 During a massive tug-of-war in Taiwan in 1997, the rope snapped and completely severed the left arms of two separate men, Yang Chiung-ming and Chen Ming-kuo.

3 Despite the fact that tug-of-war is popular internationally, there is no international governing body for the sport. Previous attempts to create one have failed, thanks to disagreement over the sport's rules. The most notable is TOWEL (the Tug-of-War Earth League), which was begun by comedian and tug-of-war aficionado Scott Thompson. TOWEL has never caught on.

1 **Fact.** De Zubiera played in the games as part of the French rugby team but decided to participate in tug-of-war as well. Tug-of-war was actually an official sport from 1900 to 1920.

2 **Fact.** There were an estimated 1,600 participants in the tug-of-war, which was part of the Retrocession Day celebration in Taipei. When the contest began, an estimated 175,000 pounds of force was applied to the rope, which immediately snapped. It's believed that Yang and Chen lost their arms when the rope rebounded with astonishing force. Both left arms were severed below the shoulder. Amazingly, after hours of surgery, both men had their arms successfully reattached.

3 # Bullsh*t!

There is an international governing body for tug-of-war, which is called the Tug of War International Federation (TWIF). Over fifty countries are members of the TWIF, from Australia to Zambia and Iran to Ukraine.

"FACTS":
Synchronized Swimming!

1 In modern times, the first organized synchronized swimming was called water ballet and was performed in lakes, rivers, and decorative water tanks, in addition to swimming pools. In the first official competitions, only men were allowed to compete.

2 In Olympic competition, the women's synchronized swimming is scored based on grace, agility, and precise timing, whereas the men's synchronized swimming is scored based on power, agility, and precise timing.

3 Synchronized swimming has an unlikely honorary founding father: Benjamin Franklin. Franklin was a proponent of physical fitness and an avid swimmer who sometimes performed feats and stunts in the water to impress onlookers.

1 **Fact.** It's funny to think that a sport that is now so thoroughly dominated by women was invented by men. The first official competition in Berlin in 1891 featured only men. But many credit a particular woman for truly popularizing the sport in the modern age. Australian-born Annette Kellermann had the perfect background to be the mother of modern synchronized swimming: She had been both a competitive distance swimmer and a ballet dancer. In 1907, she performed in a giant water tank in the New York Hippodrome and was an instant sensation. Afterward, interest in organized water ballet spread extremely quickly. That said, dancing in the water is likely as old a practice as dancing in general. There is historical evidence of in-water performances in ancient Greece and Rome, as well as ancient Japan.

2 # Bullsh*t!

Men cannot compete in Olympic synchronized swimming competitions. Nor can they compete in world championship competitions, although they are allowed to dip their toes into other international competitions.

3 **Fact.** Franklin was living proof that an athlete doesn't necessarily have to look like the Greek Titan Atlas. He was posthumously inducted into the International Swimming Hall of Fame, and he penned his own tome on the art of swimming: *The Art of Swimming Rendered Easy; With Directions to Learners. To Which Is Prefixed, Advice to Bathers.*

"FACTS":
Karate!

1 Though karate is a Japanese martial art, it was invented by non-Japanese people. It was first called *te*, but when it was later influenced by martial artists from China, it was called *kara te*, which translated to "Chinese hand."

2 In 2009, the International Olympic Committee (IOC) made karate an official Olympic sport. The only other Olympic martial art is judo.

3 While Chuck Norris won many karate championships, he has never been a karate fighter. Norris primarily studied a Korean martial art called Tang Soo Do. Now Norris is the founder of his own martial art, Chun Kuk Do, which is studied around the world.

1 **Fact.** A cultural exchange between China and Okinawa in the fourteenth century brought a whole settlement of Chinese families to the island. Practitioners of *te* began to exchange ideas and styles with practitioners of kung fu, and *kara te*, meaning "Chinese hand," was born. Okinawa was officially annexed by Japan in the nineteenth century. Today, the official Japanese translation for *karate* is "empty hand," since *karate* is a homophone that can mean both "Chinese hand" and "empty hand." It's likely they didn't like the fact that such a popular martial art was named after the Chinese. In Japan, the word is often elongated to *kara-te-dō*, which means "the way of the empty hand."

2

Bullsh*t!

The IOC has considered karate for inclusion on multiple occasions but never approved it. Beginning in 1964, judo was the only Olympic martial art, but it was joined by tae kwon do in 2000. The IOC is mum about their repeated denial of karate. A prominent theory is that the sport is too political and that major karate organizations would not be able to agree on unified rules.

3 **Fact.** Chun Kuk Do was founded in 1990 by Norris and is based on Korean martial arts styles. Norris incorporates his personal philosophy into the teaching of Chun Kuk Do, and students are exposed to his philosophical code, which includes "I will maintain an attitude of open-mindedness" and "I will always remain loyal to my God, my country, family, and my friends."

"FACTS":
The Jockstrap!

1 The word "jock," meaning "athlete," is derived from "jock-strap." The "jock" in "jockstrap" is an abbreviation of "jockey." In the late nineteenth century, cyclists were called jockeys, and the jockstrap was invented for them.

2 In the early twentieth century, the Sears catalogue sold the Heidelberg Electric Belt, a jockstrap that delivered current to the genitals. The electricity was purported to "reduce anxiety" and solve a variety of other ailments.

3 In Middletown, Connecticut, the police department has been unsuccessful in its pursuit of the "Jock-strap Bandit." The unidentified man has committed an estimated seventeen armed robberies while wearing nothing but a mask, tennis shoes, and a jockstrap. Much to the chagrin of local authorities, the man has become a cult hero among area high school and university students.

1 **Fact.** Take heart in the fact that when you refer to an athlete as a "jock," you are in effect calling that person a "jockstrap."

2 **Fact.** The Heidelberg belt was truly a marvel of science! It claimed to cure "weakness, exhaustion, impotency, rheumatism, sciatica, lame back, railroad back, insomnia, melancholia, kidney disorder, Bright's disease, dyspepsia, disorders of the liver, female weakness, poor circulation, weak heart action, and almost every known disease and weakness." Considering all that it could do, it's a wonder that it's not still on the market.

3 # Bullsh*t!
That's a total fabrication. It would lead to a pretty funny police lineup, however!

"FACTS":
The Sports Bra!

1 The first sports bra, invented in 1977 by Lisa Lindahl, was made from two jockstraps sewn together and called the Jockbra. After a booming mail-order business, her company was purchased by Playtex.

2 A popular sports bra from the early 2010s (with copycat versions still available today) is the Wine Rack, which has a built-in bladder that you can fill with the beverage of your choice. A concealable rubber tube lets you sip away at the contents wherever you are. The makers insisted that the Wine Rack can hold an entire bottle of wine.

3 Champion's Vapor sports bra incorporates a moisture-wicking fabric from an unlikely source: the cocoa tree. Structural fibers from the tree itself are woven into the fabric, prompting a popular nickname: "the chocolate bra."

1 **Fact.** According to Lindahl, her sister Victoria complained to her about soreness after jogging and quipped, "Why isn't there a jockstrap for women?" Immediately, Lindahl's idea was born. She sewed together a bra out of two jockstraps, tested it out, and dubbed it the Jockbra. She later amended it to the Jogbra, since jogging was an enormous craze in the '70s. She did a landslide mail-order business and successfully marketed it to some stores. Eventually, Playtex bought the Jogbra company from Lindahl.

2 **Fact.** This is not a sports bra that you should wear while jogging. The company that was behind the product, Cooler Fun, also made the Beer Belly—a refillable plastic beverage-holder that men can conceal under their shirts. You can find copycat versions of the Rack or the Belly still available online.

3 # Bullsh*t!

The Vapor sports bra uses Cocona fabric, which is made from coconuts, and has several desirable qualities: evaporative cooling, odor absorption, and UV protection. Unfortunately, Champion no longer makes this bra.

"FACTS":
Ping-Pong!

1 Table tennis was first invented in Chicago in the 1850s. In those early days, the ball was made of tin, but when that proved too soft, it was replaced by a bronze alloy.

2 According to the International Table Tennis Federation (ITTF), a regulation ball must be 2.7 grams in weight and 40 millimeters in diameter. The ball can only be white or orange, with a matte finish. Official competition balls are stored for three days at 73.4°F and then rigorously tested for bounce, veer, and hardness.

3 Unlike their finicky rules regarding the ball, the ITTF doesn't care what the table is made out of as long as the ball bounces to a certain height when dropped on it.

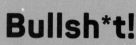

Bullsh*t!

1 The first "table tennis" patent was issued to David Foster in England in 1890. The sport had been played casually in England with improvised equipment during the previous decade. Foster's version used a cloth-covered rubber ball and actual strung rackets!

2 **Fact.** The federation is very serious about ball suitability. There is an equipment committee, with a doctor in charge of it, and they use all kinds of electrical, computer, and machine equipment to test Ping-Pong balls.

3 **Fact.** According to the federation, the table can be made of any material as long as a ball dropped from a height of 30 centimeters (not quite 12 inches) bounces about 23 centimeters (a little over 9 inches). The ball used must meet their exacting standards.

"FACTS":
Weight Lifting!

1 The word "dumbbell" comes from eighteenth-century England; athletes would remove the clappers from church bells and exercise with them. The earliest-known versions of the dumbbell were rounded stones with handles called *halteres*, which were used for athletic training in ancient Greece.

2 The current all-time records for heaviest bench press and heaviest back lift both belong to Polish strongman Konstantynów Szczytniki, who in 2022 benched 1,650 pounds. The following day, he stunned onlookers by hoisting 6,700 pounds on his back, earning him a Guinness World Record.

3 In 1990, hoping to capitalize on and repeat his success with the World Wrestling Federation, Vince McMahon launched the World Bodybuilding Federation (WBF). In the organization, bodybuilders (called BodyStars) were given colorful personalities and backstories similar to professional wrestlers.

1 **Fact.** A bell without its clapper would be mute, or "dumb" (which also used to mean mute, but is now politically incorrect), hence the name "dumbbell." When actual dumbbells began to be made, the name stuck. The *halteres* began as weights to help long jumpers train and eventually came to be used in the same manner as we use dumbbells today. At least 2,000 years ago, villagers in India began using club-shaped weights called *nals* for training.

2 # Bullsh*t!

No man walks the earth who is that great—yet. Konstantynów and Szczytniki are both places in Poland. The all-time heaviest bench-press record belongs to Jimmy Kolb, who lifted 1,350 pounds in 2023, and the all-time heaviest back-lift record belongs to Gregg Ernst, who lifted 5,340 pounds in 1993.

3 **Fact.** Unfortunately, the WBF was a dismal failure and was disbanded in 1992.

"FACTS":
Pillow Fighting!

1 The Toronto-based Pillow Fight League was a semiprofessional sports league of female competitors. Its regular events drew huge crowds and were featured on national TV. Popular fighters included Apocalipstick, Bobbi Pinn, and Olivia Neutron-Bomb. There appears to be a new league called the Pillow Fight Championship, inviting a more inclusive group of participants—not just women.

2 On April 3, 2009, President Barack Obama and First Lady Michelle Obama posed in a mock pillow-fight photo op on the South Lawn of the White House. The first family armed themselves with pillows to be photographed with fourteen-year-old Holly Bingham-Greene, who was being honored for saving her father's life.

3 A 1905 *The New York Times* headline read, "Ziegler Heir Recovers: Wealthy Boy Received His Injuries in a Pillow Fight."

1   **Fact.** The Pillow Fight League sprang up out of organized pillow-fighting nights at a goth club in Toronto. It grew steadily and even sold TV producing rights to its events. Official rules included "Female fighters only. No exceptions" and "Pillow fighters must practice good sportswomanship. No rude, lewd, or suggestive behavior." It disbanded in 2011. Recently, the Pillow Fight Championship has garnered attention; and its wealth of different participants and detailed rule set may help it stick around for longer.

2 # Bullsh*t!

There's not a single piece of truth in that statement at all. It's a total fabrication.

3   **Fact.** William Ziegler Jr. received his injuries playing with two schoolmates, and he recovered in "splendid condition," according to his physician.

"FACTS":
Strange Sports!

1 A popular sport in Finland called wife carrying now has devotees worldwide. In the event, a man carries a woman through several hundred yards of an obstacle course to win a prize, often the wife's weight in beer. The most popular method employed is the Estonian carry, in which the woman hangs upside-down with her legs around the man's head.

2 The annual cheese-rolling competition in the Cotswolds region of England has been going on for more than two centuries. In the event, competitors chase a 7-to-8-pound double Gloucester cheese wheel down a steep hill. The person first to either catch it or cross the finish line wins the cheese after which they so valiantly chased.

3 Provided you're willing to travel, and perhaps risk life and limb, you could compete this year in any of the following sports: horizontal hurdles, kite-burping, diagonal lacrosse, lake checkers, face-wrestling, finger karate, and limousine-rolling.

1 **Fact.** The sport, called *eukonkanto* in Finland, is gaining popularity worldwide. There are wife-carrying competitions in Finland, India, the UK, Germany, and the United States. It's seen as both a sports competition and party for the athletes and spectators alike.

2 **Fact.** The event attracts hundreds of fans and tourists a year. In theory, the competitors are attempting to catch the cheese, but with a one-second head start and rolling speeds as high as 70 miles per hour, catching an actively rolling cheese in the event is almost impossible (though Australian Caleb Stalder did in 2013). The competition takes place at Cooper's Hill in Gloucester, a hill so steep that major injuries are common. In the early '40s, thanks to food rationing, wooden cheese wheels were used, with tiny bits of cheese placed inside.

3 # Bullsh*t!
Those are all things that should be sports. But you could compete in these: the vertical marathon, coffin racing, nettle eating, dog surfing, swamp football, chess boxing, toe wrestling, and dead goat polo.

CHAPTER SIX

Florilegium, Omnium-Gatherum, and Gallimaufry

"FACTS":
The
Toothbrush!

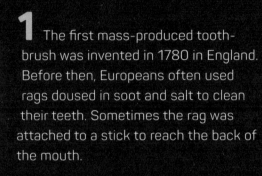

1 The first mass-produced tooth-brush was invented in 1780 in England. Before then, Europeans often used rags doused in soot and salt to clean their teeth. Sometimes the rag was attached to a stick to reach the back of the mouth.

2 In the nineteenth century, toothbrushes were often made of bone, and the bristles were actual animal hair. Horsehair, badger hair, and pig hair were all commonly used.

3 A toothbrush may seem like small potatoes when you throw it away, but environmental groups estimate 1 million pounds of plastic toothbrushes wind up in US landfills in a given year. Laid end to end, that's enough toothbrushes to stretch from Chicago to Moscow.

1 **Fact.** To this day, there are people who advocate using soot as a (very abrasive) way to whiten teeth!

2 **Fact.** The most expensive bristles were made from badger hair; horse and pig hair were also common. Synthetic bristles did not become standard until the 1940s.

3 # Bullsh*t!

Believe it or not, the actual estimate is 50 million pounds of toothbrushes per year. While 10 million pounds of toothbrushes end to end would easily circumnavigate the globe, 50 million pounds is enough to circle the planet five and three-quarters times. Two years' worth of discarded toothbrushes could reach the moon.

"FACTS":
Toilet Paper!

1 In the US, a household of four will, on average, use two trees' worth of toilet paper per year.

2 The first documented use of toilet paper in human history was in China in the sixth century c.e. By the ninth century c.e., using toilet paper was common in China (which is where paper was invented).

3 The inventor of modern commercially available toilet paper in the US was an entrepreneur named Henry Joy. Joy's Therapeutic Paper was introduced in 1740 and was rolled up on thin wooden rods in packages of three.

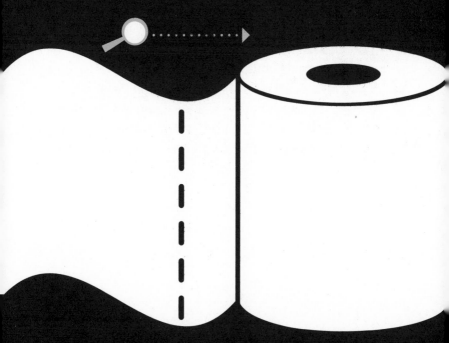

1 **Fact.** The average American uses about 50 pounds of toilet and tissue paper per year. An average-sized tree will produce around 100 pounds of toilet paper. The math checks out. If every household in the US traded out one roll of virgin toilet paper for recycled, we would, according to some experts, save 470,000 trees.

2 **Fact.** In c.e. 851, a traveler to China observed, "They [the Chinese] are not careful about cleanliness, and they do not wash themselves with water when they have done their necessities; but they only wipe themselves with paper." The ancient Egyptians were the first to use papyrus (around 3500 b.c.e.), but the Chinese were the first to make paper (c.e. 105). Paper-making did not become common practice in Europe until around c.e. 1400.

3 **Bullsh*t!**
Commercially packed toilet paper in the US did not arrive until 1857, courtesy of Joseph Gayetty. It was called Gayetty's Medicated Paper and sold in stacks of flat sheets, each one watermarked with Gayetty's name. The first rolled paper was produced by the Scott Paper Company in 1879.

"FACTS":
Stonehenge!

1 Several of the monuments that comprise Stonehenge are tripetroids, or combinations of three stones, two standing upright, with a third lying flat on top of them. The fact they remain in place after thousands of years, with the stones lying loosely on top, is an architectural marvel.

2 A henge is a Neolithic piece of earthwork consisting of a man-made circular or oval-shaped bank, with a corresponding ditch running inside it. Stonehenge would be by far the world's most famous henge, except that its name is a misnomer: It is not a true henge at all.

3 In 1905, the Ancient Order of Druids held a massive ceremony at Stonehenge, initiating over 250 new members, much to the consternation of locals. The "druids" dressed the part: They wore long white robes and fake beards.

1) Bullsh*t!

It may appear that each flat stone, or lintel, is just laying freely on top, but it is actually connected to the two uprights, or posts, with complex jointing. The lintels at Stonehenge are connected to the posts with mortise-and-tenon joints, which are basically knobs sticking up from the posts that fit into holes in the lintels. In the outer ring, the lintels are even joined, with tongue-and-groove joints. The freestanding structures of two posts and one lintel are called trilithons.

2 **Fact.** Stonehenge does have a raised bank and a ditch, but the ditch runs outside of the bank, which means it is not actually a henge. Stone monuments are not required for something to be a henge either. There are true henges with and without stones. It is totally silly that Stonehenge is not classified as a henge because the word itself is derived from the name "Stonehenge."

3 **Fact.** The Ancient Order of Druids is a London fraternal organization that was founded in 1781 (not particularly ancient, after all) and still operates today. The society is an example of neo-druidism. The press ridiculed the 1905 gathering, particularly the costumes, and huge crowds of onlookers cheered and poked fun at the earnest disciples. Many locals were vexed by the ceremony.

"FACTS":
New Jersey!

1 Most of New Jersey lies within the New York and Philadelphia metropolitan areas, and as of 2022, it is the most densely populated US state (and has been for decades).

2 About 250 million years ago, the land that is now New Jersey was immediately adjacent to the land that is now the western Sahara desert in Africa. New Jersey still contains rocks from the African plate.

3 The New Jersey state bird is the ruffed grouse, its state dance is the polka, the state animal is the white-tailed deer, and the official state song is "I'm from New Jersey."

1 **Fact.** The District of Columbia is much more densely populated than New Jersey, but it is not a state, so it doesn't qualify. As of 2022, with nearly 1,300 people per square mile, the Garden State is definitely the most densely populated. A metropolitan area is a major urban region linked socially and economically. Even though New York City is unquestionably in New York state, twelve New Jersey counties are part of the New York metropolitan area and five are in the Philadelphia metropolitan area (an additional three are on the fence). There are twenty-one counties in New Jersey.

2 **Fact.** Geologists have proven that some 250 million years ago, during the Paleozoic and Mesozoic eras, all of the earth's continents were joined into one supercontinent, often called Pangaea. Rifts formed, and the continent split into the several continents we recognize on maps today. Our continents are still moving. When Africa and New Jersey split, chunks of the African plate remained fused to New Jersey. When you stand on the New Jersey coast, you are standing on top of rocks that were once part of Africa.

3 # Bullsh*t!

The ruffed grouse, the polka, and the white-tailed deer are the state bird, dance, and animal of Pennsylvania. New Jersey is the only state that does not have a state song. Some people consider "I'm from New Jersey" to be the state song, but officially, it is not.

"FACTS":
Severed Feet!

1 A family dog from Russellville, Alabama, made national headlines in 2008 for bringing home the severed foot of a child. Police went into high alert, searching surrounding areas with cadaver-sniffing dogs and consulting numerous missing child databases. The panic immediately ceased a couple of days later when forensic test results showed that the foot was actually a bear paw.

2 Between August 2007 and December 2010, detached human feet were discovered along the coastline of Washington state and British Columbia on ten separate occasions. The majority of feet discovered were wearing socks and tennis shoes.

3 The foot of a nine-year-old Chinese girl named Ming Li was severed in July 2010 when she was run over by a tractor on her way to school. Surgeons found the foot to be too damaged to reattach straightaway, so they grafted it to her other leg to let it heal. An entire month later, they successfully reattached her foot to its proper place.

1 **Fact.** Police chief Chris Hargett hastened to point out that the paw resembled a foot closely enough that it fooled an orthopedic surgeon.

2 **Fact.** The first foot, discovered on August 20, 2007, was a right male foot in a Campus shoe. The second foot, found on August 26, 2007, was a right male foot in a Reebok. The third foot, found on February 8, 2008, was a right male foot in a Nike. The fourth foot, found on May 22, 2008, was a right female foot in a New Balance. The fifth foot, found on June 16, 2008, was a left male foot that was DNA matched with the third foot. The sixth foot, found on August 1, 2008, was a right male foot in an Everest shoe. The seventh foot, found on November 11, 2008, was a left female foot that was DNA matched with the fourth foot. The eighth foot, found on October 27, 2009, was a bare right male foot. The ninth foot, found on August 27, 2010, was a bare right foot belonging to a woman or a child. The tenth foot, found on December 5, 2010, was a right male foot in a hiking boot.

3 # Bullsh*t!

The story is close to the truth, but the reality is even cooler. Ming Li lost not her foot but her hand in the accident. The left hand was grafted to her right calf while it healed, and it was successfully reattached to her wrist three months later.

"FACTS": The White House!

1 African-American enslaved people helped build the White House. President John Adams, the first to move into the White House, was against enslaving others, so his staff contained no enslaved people.

2 The White House has a tennis court, a putting green, a billiards room, a jogging track, a swimming pool, and a bowling alley, thanks to Presidents Theodore Roosevelt, Dwight Eisenhower, John Quincy Adams, Bill Clinton, Gerald Ford, and Richard Nixon, respectively.

3 The White House has exactly eighty-eight rooms on four levels, including sixteen bathrooms. There are 198 doors, 100 windows, six fireplaces, three staircases, and an elevator. The original walls of the White House were built out of white limestone (that's how it got its name), and it takes 280 gallons of paint to cover its outside surface.

1 **Fact.** The workers themselves represent a slice of American cultural history. Many were enslaved people, many were immigrants, and some were free African Americans. Our second president, John Adams, was the first to live in the White House, and he never owned an enslaved person.

2 **Fact.** Teddy Roosevelt had tennis courts built behind the West Wing in 1902. Eisenhower had the first putting green installed outside the Oval Office. John Quincy Adams put the first billiards table in the White House in 1825, but certainly not the last. Clinton had a jogging track built around the south grounds during his first term. Gerald Ford built an outdoor swimming pool on the South Lawn in 1975. President Nixon was an avid bowler, and friends had a one-lane alley built for him in a White House basement room in 1969–1970. The alley remains!

3 # Bullsh*t!

In the White House, there are 132 rooms on six levels, including thirty-five bathrooms. There are 412 doors, 147 windows, twenty-eight fireplaces, eight staircases, and three elevators. The original walls of the White House were built out of gray sandstone, and they are still in place. "The White House" became a nickname for the house in the early nineteenth century when it was painted white, and it became the official name after Theodore Roosevelt proclaimed it so in 1901. It takes 570 gallons of paint to cover the White House's surface.

"FACTS":
Holy Cow!

1 The phrase "holy cow!" started to find common usage in the 1930s but was popularized by baseball announcers in the decades after—particularly in the '50s and '60s by broadcasting legend Phil Rizzuto, who used the phrase prodigiously. When the former Yankees shortstop's number was retired in a 1985 ceremony, an actual cow wearing a halo was brought onstage.

2 In many Hindu traditions, the cow is regarded as holy. Cows are seen as symbols of sacrifice, wealth, and strength. The 1,500-year-old *Mahabharata* says, "Cows are the foremost of all things...there is nothing more sacred or sanctifying than cows."

3 If you look closely at the chandelier hanging in the middle of the Massachusetts Senate chamber, you'll notice that a brass casting of a cow is incorporated into it. The casting is fondly nicknamed "the Holy Cow," and also has a counterpart in the House of Representatives chamber in the Massachusetts State House in the form of a painted cow portrait. The painting was famously stolen in 1933 by members of the *Harvard Lampoon* in an incident called the "Cow-Napping."

1 **Fact.** Rizzuto's exclamations of "holy cow!" punctuated many dramatic moments in Yankees history and led to multiple cow-themed tributes to the man. At the 1985 ceremony, the live "holy" cow accidentally (and comically) knocked Rizzuto off his feet.

2 **Fact.** In traditional Hindu societies, even the vegetarians derive a lot of benefit from cows. Milk, curds, and ghee (clarified butter) provide the basis for their diet. Cows perform labor by pulling carts and plows. Even cow dung has its uses: It is an excellent fuel when burned, and because it contains ammonia and menthol, burning dung repels mosquitoes and even acts as a disinfectant. That cows provide all these things is seen as the embodiment of merit.

3 # Bullsh*t!

There is no cow in that chandelier, and there was no "cow-napping." However, there is a brass casting of a fish incorporated into the chandelier in the Massachusetts Senate chamber, which is colloquially known as the "Holy Mackerel." It's believed to be the counterpart to the Sacred Cod, a 1784 carving of a codfish that hangs in the House of Representatives chamber. The Sacred Cod was famously pilfered in 1933 by members of the *Harvard Lampoon* in an incident known as the "Cod-Napping." It was returned two days later after members of the House refused to legislate without the cod present.

"FACTS":
1950!

1 In 1950, President Truman ended racial segregation in the military, Israel declared its independence, and the Republic of Korea was established.

2 In 1950, *South Pacific* won the Pulitzer Prize for Drama and the Tony Award for Best Musical. The Academy Award for Best Picture went to *All the King's Men*. The first *Peanuts* and *Beetle Bailey* comic strips appeared in newspapers.

3 In 1950, the United States population was 152,271,417. The average household income was $4,237. There were slightly more women than men, but they only made up 28.8 percent of the workforce.

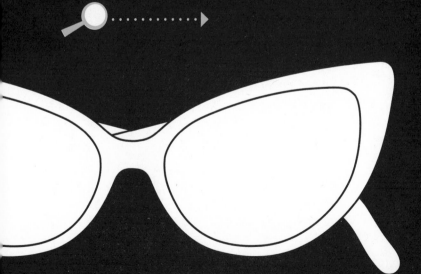

Bullsh*t!

All of those things happened in 1948.

Fact. In 1950, we also saw the first kidney transplant and the first TV remote control (it was connected to a wire). The Yankees won the World Series, and the NBA championship went to the Minneapolis Lakers.

Fact. The United States population has more than doubled since 1950, and we now make well over ten times as much money on average, although adjusting for inflation, we make about one and a third times as much money. These days, there are still more women than men, and they make up a little less than half of the workforce.

"FACTS":
Hugs!

1 A 2018 study by animal behaviorists at the DuPage Animal Hospital in Villa Park, Illinois, proved that dogs that are "routinely held, hugged, and cuddled with" are three times as likely to live longer and remain healthier than dogs that aren't. The study inspired the Humane Society to distribute bumper stickers that say, "Have you hugged your dog today?"

2 In a major new national trend, schools across the country have been instituting a new ban in hopes to keep our kids safe. The dangerous culprit from which we need to protect them? Hugs.

3 A study at the University of North Carolina concluded that hugging can lower your blood pressure. Interestingly, the effect was much more pronounced on women than men.

1 Bullsh*t!

Nothing is true in that paragraph. In fact, animal behaviorists assert that dogs don't like to be hugged, even when it's their beloved master doing the embracing. When dogs place a limb over or around another dog, or superimpose their bodies over another, it is a sign of dominance and aggression. The scientists go on to say that hugging a dog you're not familiar with is a good way to get bitten. So, next time you want to show Spot that you love him, lick his face instead.

2 **Fact.** The hug threat is being addressed at our schools with varying levels of severity, from outright bans on any form of physical contact (even the high five) to strict time limits of two or three seconds per hug.

3 **Fact.** The North Carolina study is just one of a multitude that show loving physical contact is demonstrably beneficial to health. In the study, the huggers showed decreased blood pressure long after the actual hug and even during the recounting of a stressful memory. Both men and women also showed increased levels of oxytocin, sometimes called the "love hormone," which is supposed to have a beneficial effect on the heart. The dip in blood pressure was more pronounced in women, and women also showed a clear dip in cortisol, which is known as the "stress hormone."

"FACTS":
Impostors!

1 Joshua Abraham Norton was a British-born business-
man and resident of San Francisco who, on Septem-
ber 17, 1859, declared himself emperor of the United
States. During his "reign," the "Imperial Majesty of these
United States" issued numerous decrees, ate at any
San Francisco restaurant for free, issued his own currency (which was accepted anywhere in the city), and
declared himself "Protector of Mexico."

2 In the late '90s, the St. Paul VI Catholic High School
in Fairfax, Virginia, was delighted to welcome sixteen-
year-old incoming student Jonathan Taylor Spielberg,
the rich nephew of director Steven Spielberg. Not long
into his tenure at the high school, it was revealed that
"Spielberg" was actually Anoushirvan Fakhran, a twenty-
seven-year-old former porn actor from Iran.

3 In the 1970s, Dr. Charlotte Bach taught biology at the
University of East London for three years before it was
revealed that she had never been a scientist and, in
fact, had never even earned a college degree.

1 **Fact.** The emperor was so beloved by locals that his seal of approval led to increased business for merchants (hence his free meal ticket at any restaurant) and his self-issued currency was collectible and valuable (and therefore accepted tender in San Francisco). When a local police officer arrested Norton in hopes of committing him to an asylum, locals responded with outrage. Norton was released, the police apologized, and, from then on, he was routinely saluted in the streets by the boys in blue. Norton ordered the construction of both a bridge and a tunnel across San Francisco Bay. Like all of his decrees, it was ignored, but the Transbay Tube (built in 1969) bears a plaque of "Norton I, Emperor of the United States, Protector of Mexico" to this day.

2 **Fact.** When his fakery was found out, Fakhran received an eleven-month suspended sentence and 100 hours of community service. When asked why he did it, he said, "Just for the fun, to get the experience I never had."

3 # Bullsh*t!

Dr. Charlotte Bach never taught at the University of East London. She was a fringe evolutionary theorist with a large following among scientists and intellectuals in 1970s London and was thought to be a former lecturer at Budapest's Eötvös Loránd University. Upon her death in 1981, it was revealed that Dr. Charlotte Bach was never a scientist or a professor and indeed was never Dr. Charlotte Bach: She was actually born Karoly Hajdu, and was a Hungarian immigrant and former criminal.

"FACTS":
Rare Books!

1 The most expensive printed book ever sold was a copy of *The Bay Psalm Book*, which was purchased at auction in 2013 for $14.2 million. The most expensive manuscript ever sold was Leonardo da Vinci's handwritten *Codex Leicester*, which Bill Gates bought in 1994 for $30.8 million.

2 The libraries of both Brown and Harvard Universities contain books bound in human skin.

3 The Voynich manuscript, a handwritten book on 240 vellum pages from the early fifteenth century, and contains essays on natural history, religion, astronomy, mysticism, and mathematics. It is believed to have been written by Matthias Voynich, who was seven years old at the time.

1 **Fact.** Only eleven copies of *The Bay Psalm Book* are thought to exist. The *Codex Leicester* contains seventy-two pages of Leonardo da Vinci's personal scientific writings and drawings. Gates scanned the document and included the images as a screen saver in Windows 95. Nice of him to share.

2 **Fact.** The practice of binding books in human skin could be found several times in human history and is known as "anthropodermic bibliopegy." Several such tomes still exist today in rare book collections, including Arsene Houssaye's *Des destinées de l'ame* in Harvard's Houghton Library that bears this inscription: "A book about the human soul deserved to have a human covering: I had kept this piece of human skin taken from the back of a woman." Creepy.

3 # Bullsh*t!

The Voynich manuscript is a handwritten book on 240 vellum pages from the early fifteenth century. As far as we know, the book was not written by a seven-year-old or anyone named Matthias. All 35,000 words are written in an unknown language with an unknown alphabet, and, since its discovery in 1912, nobody has been able to translate or decode it, including celebrated cryptographers, military code breakers, and sophisticated computers. The language does follow normal patterns of the written word (and is therefore not gibberish), but the meaning of those words is still lost on us today.

"FACTS":
Pajamas!

1 The word "pajama" is originally derived from the Persian word *paejamah*, which means "leg clothing." The word was adopted by the British during their presence in India in the eighteenth and nineteenth centuries.

2 According to a recent ABC News poll, only 10 percent of Americans wear pajamas to bed. Some 33 percent responded that they wear underwear to bed, and a whopping 48 percent responded that they wear nothing at all.

3 A Welsh supermarket caused an international stir when it instituted a strict no-pajamas policy in 2010. Customers in pj's were turned away at the door.

1 Fact. The Indian version in the nineteenth century was *pai jamahs*, which were actually loose-fitting pants. The British found them exceedingly comfortable and brought them home. Eventually, they became common sleepwear. "Pajama" is sometimes spelled "pyjama," which is the primary spelling in England and Canada.

2 Bullsh*t!

You wanted to believe it, though, right? The survey showed that 33 percent of Americans wear pajamas to bed, 23 percent wear "shorts/T-shirt," 16 percent wear underwear, 22 percent go naked, and 1 percent wear "sweatshirt/sweatpants." In the poll, 2 percent responded that they wear "something else," which one might assume includes such popular choices as astronaut suit, scuba gear, diaper, and chain mail.

3 Fact. The Tesco supermarket in Cardiff posted this rule: "To avoid causing offence or embarrassment to others we ask that our customers are appropriately dressed when visiting our store (footwear must be worn at all times and no nightwear is permitted)." BBC News interviewed at least one customer who was turned away: a full-time mother of two who was swinging by the store in her PJs. Her reaction? "I think it's stupid." The dress code ignited debates in both the UK and the US about the habit of wearing sleepwear in public and whether it should be regulated or not.

"FACTS":
Eleven!

1 Eleven is an extremely significant number in multiple religions: In Hinduism, a feast is organized on the eleventh day of death. Eleven is the number of nodes in Metatron's Cube, which is used in the Kabbalah. Eleven is the traditional number of witches in a Wiccan coven. According to the Torah, God has eleven attributes of mercy.

2 The word "eleven" comes from the German word meaning "one left over," because it's the first number that can't be counted using the fingers (and thumbs) of both hands.

3 The armistice with Germany, which ended World War I, occurred on the eleventh hour of the eleventh day of the eleventh month of the year.

11

1 Bullsh*t!

All of these statements are true of the number thirteen, not eleven.

2 **Fact.** The Old High German word is *einlif*, literally meaning "one remaining." The Old English word, meaning essentially the same thing, is *endleofan*. In case you were wondering.

3 **Fact.** The agreement between the Allies and Germany was made at 5 a.m. on November 11, 1918, but was set to go into effect at 11 a.m. The last six hours were marked by a surge in fighting, as many wanted to get in the last best shot before the cease-fire. Armistice Day, renamed Veteran's Day, is still celebrated on November 11.

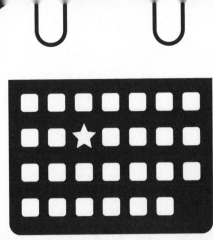

"FACTS":
Tuesday!

1 In English, Tuesday gets its name from a one-handed god of war in Norse mythology. In most Romance languages, Tuesday is named after the Roman god of war.

2 Fat Tuesday has been observed annually in New Orleans since its founding as the capital of French Louisiana in 1702, making it the oldest Fat Tuesday celebration in America.

3 Keith Richards wrote the Rolling Stones song "Ruby Tuesday" about a groupie named Linda Keith, who quit following the band and later became involved with Jimi Hendrix. The Ruby Tuesday restaurant chain is named after the song.

1 **Fact.** "Tuesday" comes from "Tiw's Day," and *Tiw* is the Old English version of the Norse *Týr*. Týr was a warrior from the Norse pantheon, who was associated with combat, tactics, law, and victory. The legend says that Týr sacrificed his hand to the great wolf Fenrir. Mars was the Roman god of war and is often identified as an analogue of Týr. "Tiw's Day" may have been a translation of the Latin *dies Martis*, or "Day of Mars." Tuesday in most Romance languages is named after *Martis*, such as the French *mardi*, Spanish *martes*, Italian *martedì*, Catalan *dimarts*, and Romanian *marţi*. Even the Irish use it: *dé máirt*. Other languages prefer Týr over Mars, as English does, such as the Danish *tirsdag*, Swedish *tisdag*, and Finnish *tiistai*. In either case, Tuesday is a good day to do battle.

2 # Bullsh*t!

New Orleans wasn't founded until 1718. Mobile was founded as the capital of French Louisiana in 1702, even though it is now, of course, firmly in Alabama. Mobile's original Fat Tuesday (which translated into French is *mardi gras*) celebrations were the first in America and continue to this day.

3 **Fact.** Keith Richards said the song was "about Linda Keith not being there. She had p*ssed off somewhere. It was very mournful...and it was a Tuesday." The first Ruby Tuesday restaurant was founded in 1972, five years after "Ruby Tuesday" was released and hit number one on the music charts.

"FACTS":
Pink!

1 We call our little fingers "pinkies" because, with young children, the little finger is often the rosiest.

2 Before the 1930s, it was commonly held in the United States that blue was for girls and pink was for boys.

3 In the seventeenth century, if you sent your sheets to be dyed pink, you'd be very likely to get them back bearing a rich shade of yellow.

1 Bullsh*t!

We get the word "pinky" (or "pinkie") from the Dutch word *pink*, which means "little finger."

2 **Fact.** Pink, as a shade of red, was thought to be a bolder color, more suitable for masculinity. Blue, which is associated with the Virgin Mary, was thought to be soft and feminine. In a 1918 issue of *Ladies' Home Journal*, you can find this passage: "The generally accepted rule is pink for the boy and blue for the girl. The reason is that pink being a more decided and stronger colour is more suitable for the boy, while blue, which is more delicate and daintier, is prettier for the girl."

3 **Fact.** Back then, "pink" or "pinke" referred to the pigment extracted from unripe buckthorn berries, which was similar in shade to goldenrod yellow. The pigment is now called "stil de grain yellow." "Pink" did not become the widespread word for the cotton candy color we know and love until the eighteenth century.

"FACTS":
Feline Cruelty!

1 In a top secret 1967 experiment, the CIA surgically implanted a set of microphones and a battery into a cat, and an antenna in its tail, hoping to use the poor animal for spy missions. In its first test mission, operatives directed the cat to eavesdrop on a pair of men outside of the Soviet compound in Washington, DC. As soon as the cat was released, it darted into the street and was promptly run over and killed by a taxi cab. The project was scrapped.

2 In late medieval France, a truly disgusting spectacle was common during midsummer festivals: cat burning. Dozens of live cats would be collected in a bag or net and suspended over a bonfire. Revelers collected the ashes afterward, believing them to be good luck.

3 In the 1940 Soviet "science" film *Experiments in the Revival of Organisms*, the severed head of a cat is shown to be kept alive by receiving a steady supply of oxygenated blood from an artificial heart and lung simulator called an autojector. The head responds to stimuli such as being poked or brushed with a feather.

1 **Fact.** The people involved nicknamed the operation "Acoustic Kitty." Despite the $15 million price tag, the dead prototype, and the discontinuation of the project, the CIA memo reported that the experiment was a "remarkable scientific achievement" because "cats can indeed be trained to move short distances."

2 **Fact.** It's horrible, deplorable, and awful, but it's true. In 1648, King Louis XIV lit the fire himself. In many medieval societies, animals were believed to represent different sides of human nature (look up "scapegoat"), and cats had the awful luck of being associated with the evils in humanity and the devil. For that reason, burning cats was not regarded as cruel; instead, it was seen as a way to cleanse society of evil.

3 # Bullsh*t!

Is the story true? No. Is it far-fetched? No. In fact, the whole thing happened as described, except it was the head of a dog, not a cat. To this day, the scientific community doesn't know what to make of the movie. Some believe it is real and have even cited the experiments in articles and papers, and some believe it was a hoax video, made for the purposes of Soviet propaganda. Either way, it's very, very disturbing.

"FACTS":
Exploding Whales!

1 In 1970, an 8-ton sperm whale beached itself on the Oregon coast and promptly died. Cleanup fell under the jurisdiction of the Oregon Highway Division, which decided the most logical course of action was to blow it up. A thousand pounds of dynamite were strapped to the carcass and detonated.

2 In 2004, a 56-foot-long, 60-ton sperm whale beached itself on the Taiwan coast and promptly died. It took three cranes and fifty workers thirteen hours to get the carcass on the back of an eighteen-wheeler so that it could be transported to a wildlife study center. En route, in the urban center of the bustling city of Tainan, the whale exploded, showering shops, cars, and onlookers with blood and rotting entrails.

3 In 2018, a 30-foot-long humpback whale became stranded in shallow water near the Western Australia coast, prompting authorities to attempt to tow it back to safety. Before the rescue mission was underway, the whale spontaneously exploded. Nobody was injured, as the whale was safely underwater, and the carcass was towed out to sea anyway. Scientists, unable to examine the body, have offered no adequate explanation for the bizarre bursting.

1 **Fact.** The theory went that the dynamite would effectively disintegrate the massive carcass, leaving pieces small enough for scavengers to clean up. Immediately after the explosion it became apparent that the technique was not beneficial. Large pieces of whale and globs of blubber rained down on buildings and parking lots some distance away, causing damage. As for the whale, only part of it was disintegrated, leaving a massive smoking whale pile for the Oregon Highway Division to clean up.

2 **Fact.** The explosion was caused by a natural buildup of gas inside the decomposing whale. More than 600 people had gathered in the street to watch the bizarre procession, only to have their day go horribly wrong. No matter how bad a day you're having, remember, it could be worse!

3 # Bullsh*t!

In 2010, a 30-foot-long humpback whale was stranded in shallow water near the Western Australia coast, and it did explode, though not naturally. Authorities decided to euthanize the trapped animal by blowing it up.

"FACTS":
The Pencil!

1 The world's largest pencil is 76 feet long, weighs 22,000 pounds, and contains 4,000 pounds of Pennsylvania graphite. It was built by Ashrita Furman, who has set more than six hundred Guinness World Records in his lifetime.

2 Though he's remembered primarily as a philosopher, Henry David Thoreau was also an inventor, and he often included the words "civil engineer" after his name. His father was a pencil maker, and Thoreau was an avid participant in the business, designing a pencil-making technique that turned the business into a wild success.

3 Ernest Hemingway and Jack Kerouac were avid pencil pushers, using the implement to write their books. Hemingway sometimes went through sixty pencils in one day. Cormac McCarthy wrote all his books exclusively in pencil.

1 **Fact.** One of Furman's records is for "the most current Guinness World Records held at the same time by an individual." Furman's records are eclectic, such as the "fastest mile balancing a milk bottle on his head," a record that he set while in Indonesia in 2004. Furman's enormous pencil cost $20,000 to produce and beat the 65-foot pencil that sits outside of pencil maker Faber-Castell's headquarters in Malaysia.

2 **Fact.** Thoreau spent a lot of his adult life pitching in to the family business. He discovered a way to mix inferior graphite with clay to make a smooth-writing pencil of any hardness desired. The result was a booming pencil company. Of course, Thoreau being Thoreau, he walked away from the success and sought no personal gain from the invention.

3 **Bullsh*t!**

Hemingway and Kerouac favored the typewriter, as did McCarthy. In 2009, McCarthy's typewriter, on which he believed he wrote 5 million words, sold at auction for $254,500. John Steinbeck was a pencil fanatic, sometimes going through sixty pencils in one day. It is said that he would start each writing day with twenty-four sharpened pencils, which he would need to resharpen before the day was out. He used 300 pencils while writing *East of Eden*.

"FACTS":
Laughter!

1 Chimpanzees, bonobos, gorillas, orangutans, dogs, and rats all laugh.

2 On average, children laugh at least ten times as often as adults on a daily basis. Laughter can lower your blood pressure, reduce pain, increase vascular blood flow, and improve your ability to learn.

3 People laugh most frequently at funny jokes.

1 **Fact.** Ape laughter sounds quite different from a person's (like a combination between breathing and shrieking), but it is definitely present in both captive and wild apes during tickling and horseplay. Dog laughter sounds to us like heavy panting, but the pattern is quite different from what you'd hear from an out-of-breath dog. Dogs laugh when they play, and research has proven that the sound of a dog laughing elicits a play response in other nearby dogs. Scientists have proven that rats are ticklish, and while being tickled or engaged in rough-and-tumble play, they emit ultrasonic vocalization patterns that seem to be primitive laughter.

2 **Fact.** Multiple studies have consistently proven that laughter provides a whole host of health benefits. Unfortunately, laughter can also kill. Laughter can cause atony (muscle failure), which can lead to syncope (fainting), which in turn can put you in jeopardy. In one reported case, a Danish man died during a laughing fit while watching the movie *A Fish Called Wanda*.

3 # Bullsh*t!
People actually don't laugh very often at jokes. Most laughter is a result of human interaction and conversation, as a whole.

Index

R

Rolling Stones, 241–42
Rubik's Cube, 53–54

S

Sandwiches, 109–10
Science, weird, 6, 131–70
Severed feet, 223–24
Shakespeare, William, 87–88
Sharks, 39–40
Sleep, 9–10, 25–26, 41–42, 107
Spam, 129–30
Sports, 6, 171–212
Sports bra, 203–4
Squirrels, 47–48
Star Trek, 61–62
Star Wars, 59–60
Stonehenge, 219–20
Strange sports, 211–12. *See also* Sports
Sun, 133–34, 157, 170
Supercalifragilisticexpialidocious, 83–84
Superman, 81–82
Supernova, 133–34
Swans, 35–36
Sweeteners, 99–100, 123–26
Sweets, 93–94, 113–14, 117–18, 121–28
Swimming, synchronized, 197–98

T

Table tennis, 205–6
Tequila, 111–12
Tetris, 65–66
Tigers, 43–44
Toads, 17–18
Toilet paper, 217–18
Tomatoes, 91–92
Toothbrushes, 215–16
Toys, 53–54, 159–60, 185–88
Tuesdays, 241–42
Tug-of-war, 195–96

Twinkies, 127–28
Tyrannosaurus, 33–34

U

Unicorn, 45–46
Uranus, 169–70
Urine, 139–42

V

Vegetables, 91–92, 106
Viagra, 23–24, 155–56
Video games, 65–66, 68, 71–72
Volleyball, 179–80

W

Watermelon, 105–6
Wedgies, 75–76
Weight lifting, 207–8
Weird science, 6, 131–70
Whale sharks, 39–40
Whales, exploding, 247–48
White House, 107–8, 209, 225–26
Wine, 95–96, 120, 203
Words, longest, 83–84
Worms, 27–28, 111–12, 151–52

Y

Yo-yos, 185–86

Z

Zombies, 67–68

ABOUT THE AUTHOR

Neil Patrick Stewart
is an actor, director, and writer.
He holds an MFA in acting from the
world-renowned American Repertory
Theater/Moscow Art Theatre (ART/MXAT)
Institute for Advanced Theater Training at Harvard
University. Neil is the associate artistic director of
The Performing Arts Project and a faculty member
at Texas State University. He's written hundreds of
magazine articles, ghostwritten a book or two, performed
as an actor all over the world, worked as a chef,
personal assistant, voiceover artist, volleyball coach,
painter, comedian, audition coach, cashier, copyeditor,
emcee, mover, theater director, life coach, box office
employee, babysitter, speaker, dancer, bookstore
clerk, pasta slinger, and a teacher of carpentry to
kindergarteners (that one lasted less than a
week). He lives in San Marcos, Texas, with
his wife, Lynzy, his son, Rocket, and
his dogs, Puzzle and Gravy.